Student Learning Outside the Classroom:
Transcending Artificial Boundaries

by George D. Kuh, Katie Branch Douglas, Jon P. Lund, and Jackie Ramin-Gyurnek

ASHE-ERIC Higher Education Report No. 8, 1994

Saint Peter's University Library
Withdrawn

Prepared by

Clearinghouse on Higher Education
The George Washington University

In cooperation with

Association for the Study
of Higher Education

Published by

Graduate School of Education and Human Development
The George Washington University

Jonathan D. Fife, Series Editor

Cite as

Kuh, George D., Douglas, Katie Branch, Lund, Jon P., Ramin Gyurnek, Jackie. 1994. *Student Learning Outside the Classroom: Transcending Artificial Boundaries.* ASHE-ERIC Higher Education Report No. 8. Washington, D.C.: The George Washington University, School of Education and Human Development.

Library of Congress Catalog card Number 96-75972
ISSN 0884-0040
ISBN 1-878380-64-8

Managing Editor: Lynne J. Scott
Manuscript Editor: Judy A. Beck
Cover Design by Michael David Brown, Rockville, Maryland

The ERIC Clearinghouse on Higher Educaton invites individuals to submit proposals for writing monographs for the *ASHE-ERIC Higher Education Report* series. Proposals must include:
1. A detailed manuscript proposal of not more than five pages.
2. A chapter-by-chapter outline.
3. A 75-word summary to be used by several review committees for the initial screening and rating of each proposal.
4. A vita and a writing sample.

ERIC Clearinghouse on Higher Education
School of Education and Human Development
The George Washington University
One Dupont Circle, Suite 630
Washington, DC 20036-1183

This publication was prepared paritally with funding from the Office of Education Research and Improvement, U.S. Departent of Education, under contract no. ED RR-93-002008. The opinions expressed in this report do not necessarily reflect the positions or policies of OERI or the Department.

LB
3605
K83
1994

EXECUTIVE SUMMARY

The 1990s constitute one of the most dynamic periods in the history of American higher education. Unpredictable economic conditions, accountability demands, demographic shifts, enrollment pressures, and heightened expectations for higher education are forcing colleges and universities to examine virtually every aspect of their operation.

The aspect of institutional functioning in which many stakeholders, including potential students, are most interested is what students gain from attending college. The Wingspread Group (1993) asserted that higher education must put student learning first. Students learn and develop in a holistic, integrated way as they engage in both academic and nonacademic activities in and outside the classroom. That is, what is most important in college is a student's total level of engagement in different types of learning activities, not where the activities occur. Institutions must find ways to encourage students to take advantage of the array of human and physical resources for learning in which institutions have already invested. One approach is to make time spent in classes more productive. However, the largest discretionary block of time for undergraduate students is outside the classroom, an area that receives little systematic attention but which has considerable potential for increasing learning (Astin 1993; Chickering and Reisser 1993; Kuh 1993; Kuh, Schuh, Whitt, and Associates 1991; Pascarella and Terenzini 1991).

What Do Out-of-Class Experiences Contribute to Valued Outcomes of College?

Following is a summary of the research on "the other curriculum," the contributions of out-of-class experiences of undergraduates to valued outcomes of postsecondary education. The literature is examined using Kuh's (1993) five-category typology: (a) cognitive complexity (e.g., critical thinking, intellectual flexibility, reflective judgment), (b) knowledge acquisition and application, (c) humanitarianism (e.g., interest in the welfare of others), (d) interpersonal and intrapersonal competence (e.g., self-confidence, identity, ability to relate to others), and (e) practical competence (e.g., decision making, vocational preparation). In addition, out-of-class experiences linked to persistence and educational attainment also are considered because the longer one persists in college the greater the gains in all of the outcome categories listed earlier (Pascarella and Terenzini 1991).

Out-of-class experiences contribute to gains in all of these areas as well as to educational attainment. Students who expend more effort in a variety of areas seem to benefit the most intellectually as well as in the personal development domain (Pascarella and Terenzini 1991). At the same time, some experiences are more likely than others to foster desired outcomes. For example, living in an academic-theme residence is associated with gains in critical thinking, intellectual development, and aesthetic appreciation. Similarly, involvement in student government has been linked to gains in student understanding and appreciation of human differences, and increases in practical competence.

Relatively few students consciously apply what they are learning in class to their lives beyond the classroom (Kuh 1993). This is unfortunate because self-knowledge and understanding result from examining social and personal values in a variety of settings.

What Conditions Foster Student Learning Outside the Classroom?

Nine institutional conditions seem to encourage students to use their out-of-class experiences to educational advantage:

1. clear, coherent, and consistently expressed educational purposes;
2. an institutional philosophy that embraces a holistic view of talent development;
3. complementary institutional policies and practices congruent with students' characteristics and needs;
4. high, clear expectations for student performance;
5. use of effective teaching approaches;
6. systematic assessment of student performance and institutional environments, policies, and practices;
7. ample opportunities for student involvement in educationally purposeful out-of-class activities;
8. human scale settings characterized by ethics of membership and care; and
9. an ethos of learning that pervades all aspects of the institution.

How Can Institutions Enhance Student Learning?
Any institution can enhance student learning by using its existing resources more effectively to create the conditions under which students learn best, both inside and outside the classroom. The key tasks in transcending the artificial boundaries are (a) to break down the barriers between various units (e.g., academic departments, administrative services, student affairs) and (b) to create situations in which students are forced to examine the connections between their studies and life outside the classroom and to apply what they are learning.

Creating the conditions that promote student learning outside the classroom consistent with an institution's educational purposes will require an institutional renewal effort designed to:

1. cultivate an ethos of learning;
2. address the importance of out-of-class experiences explicitly in the institution's mission;
3. establish a holistic approach to talent development as the institution's philosophy of undergraduate education;
4. assess periodically the impact of out-of-class environments on students;
5. develop a common view of "what matters" in undergraduate education; and
6. attempt to shape the student culture in ways that will foster responsible behavior and educationally desirable outcomes.

With this agenda in mind, various stakeholders must exercise responsibility for creating an ethos of learning that encourages students to use their out-of-class time in educationally purposeful ways.

What can governing boards do?
Governing boards positively influence student learning outside the classroom when they: support such experiences financially and in other ways; use process indicators and outcomes data in setting institutional policy; ask students what they gain from their experiences outside the classroom; and hire a president who values undergraduate education

and understands and appreciates the contributions of life outside the classroom to institutional and student goals.

What can presidents do?

The degree to which the institution values student learning outside the classroom is—in part—a function of the amount of attention the president gives to the topic. Thus, the president must have accurate information about students and their experiences, provide moral and financial support to those who are engaged with students outside the classroom in educationally purposeful activities, remind stakeholders about the value of out-of-class experiences, and hold the student affairs unit accountable for articulating the value of life outside the classroom.

What can academic administrators do?

Senior academic officers can have a substantial influence on creating an ethos of learning and promoting learning outside the classroom if they hire learning-centered faculty members, send consistent messages about the nature and complementarity of in-class and out-of-class experiences, revise tenure and promotion policies so that faculty involvement with students outside the classroom is rewarded, assess whether academic support services are meeting the needs of all students, and establish strong working relations and communication links between academic and student affairs.

What can faculty members do?

Faculty influence out-of-class learning environments by the nature and amount of academic work they assign and the learning resources they expect students to use in order to complete assignments. To link the curriculum and academic goals more closely with student life outside the classroom, faculty can structure assignments that require students to illustrate how they are using class material in other areas of their lives, use active learning and other effective pedagogical strategies, work against prevailing norms that discourage meaningful interaction with students beyond the classroom, emphasize intellectual matters and course material when interacting informally with students, hold students to high expectations, and indicate clearly what they must do to succeed academically.

What can student affairs administrators do?

Student affairs staff play a key role in promoting student involvement in educationally purposeful activities beyond the classroom when they—in partnership with the faculty—help students make connections between the curriculum and their out-of-class experiences. Thus, student affairs staff must: understand and appreciate the institution's educational purposes; translate what the institution values into behavioral terms for student life beyond the classroom; communicate clearly to academic administrators, faculty members, students, and others how life beyond the classroom contributes to desired outcomes of college; collect and disseminate data about students and their experiences; and ask students to think about, and apply, what they are learning in class to life outside the classroom, and vice versa.

What can students do?

Students take responsibility for their own learning when they use the institution's resources to educational advantage. Evidence of this is when students select an institution that takes undergraduate education seriously, attend orientation, participate in out-of-class activities and events designed to enrich the educational experience (e.g., guest lectures, off-campus programs), enroll in courses that employ active learning strategies, use resources to enhance their academic skills, evaluate the quality of their relations with peers and others, develop a portfolio of out-of-class learning experiences and associated benefits, and discuss with others their academic progress and how what they are learning in classes applies to other aspects of their life.

How Can Artificial Boundaries between Classrooms and Out-of-Class Experiences Be Transcended?

The conditions that promote student learning outside the classroom cannot be created by any one individual—president, academic or student life dean, or governing board member. However, by working together, by linking programs and activities across the academic and out-of-class dimensions of campus life, and by removing obstacles to students' pursuit of their academic and personal goals, an institution can increase the likelihood that students will experience college as a seamless web of learning across classroom and out-of-class settings. For this to occur, the institution's ethos must send the message that learning is continuous and contagious—in the biology lab, library, academic adviser's office, residence hall lounge, and student union; at a place of employment; during community service; and on the playing fields.

CONTENTS

FOREWORD

The call for greater faculty and institutional facilities productivity is a familiar one. As resources become scarcer and faculty become more expensive, there is a concern over the return on the educational investment. D. Bruce Johnstone (1993) has taken a different approach by suggesting that instead of placing responsibility, or blame, on faculty for their failure to be more productive, a more effective approach would be to concentrate on shortening the time spent in getting a degree by improving the productivity of learning. Combining this approach with the research findings that out-of-classroom experiences have a more lasting and defining impact on students than do the classroom experiences, a logical conclusion is to concentrate on what can be done to make the out-of-classroom experiences more connected with the overall education mission of the institution.

There are a number of underlying assumptions or cultural values that have kept outside-the-classroom student learning from being a more integrated part of the overall curriculum. The most obvious reasons are:

- Faculty see themselves as the primary source of a student's education. What students learn from each other or through the extracurricular process is seen as irrelevant to the formal curriculum as supervised by faculty.
- Learning primarily occurs when faculty are talking (active teaching) and students are listening (passive learning).
- Learning occurs primarily in formal setting—the classrooms and laboratories.
- Faculty teaching status is not enhanced by linking the learning in the classroom with that outside the classroom.
- The interaction of faculty with students outside the classroom is mostly voluntary and does not count significantly for promotion, tenure, or merit pay decisions.
- Faculty are responsible for what goes on in their classrooms. The combined impact of all the courses student take (the academic curriculum) and the learning outside the classroom (the total impact of a higher education experience) is someone else's responsibility.

This separation of faculty from the students' out-of-classroom experiences has developed over the last hundred years. As the research universities came into prominence and increased academic specialization was rewarded, less time and attention was available for faculty to interact with students outside the classroom. At the same time the overall education mission of institutions changed from that of educating the whole student to providing specialized degrees. What needs to occur to redirect this trend so as to gain the best of both approaches and to enhance both faculty and learning productivity is to reconceptualize the undergraduate learning experience from a series of discrete and uncoordinated happenings to a total series of experiences that work together to achieve the education mission of the institution.

In this report, written by George D. Kuh, professor of higher education; Katie Branch Douglas, a candidate in higher education and student affairs; and Jackie Ramin-Gyurnek, a visiting research associate in the Vice President's Office—all at Indiana University; and by Jon P. Lund, director of residence life at Luther College, the issue of institutional productivity and student learning outside the classroom is examined with particular focus on what is known about educational attainment and specific outcomes. The authors review the conditions that foster a climate where out-of-classroom experiences can contribute to greater educational productivity. Finally, what specific actions can be taken are discussed by roles and positions. Everyone in the institution from the governing board and president to faculty and students must accept some responsibility to work to maximize the effectiveness of the outside classroom experiences.

As the research and experiences reviewed by the authors of this Report demonstrate, those institutions that have a strong link between their formal classroom objectives and their student's out-of-class experiences have the biggest impact on their students. This was recognized in the 1970s when the Center for Research and Development in Higher Education at the University of California–Berkeley (Clark, Heist, McConnell, Trow, and Young 1972)[a] identified the "potent" colleges and when J.B. Lon Hefferlin (1971)[b] wrote about the dynamics of academic reform and what were the characteristics of high-functioning institutions in *Dynamics*

---

[a] *Students and Colleges: Interaction and Change.*
[b] San Francisco: Jossey-Bass.

of Academic Reform. More recent publications that have recognized this crucial interaction are Kuh, Schuh, Whitt, and Associates (1991)[c] and our Report by Townsend, Newell, and Wiese, *Creating Distinctiveness: Lessons from Uncommon Colleges and Universities* (1992).[d] For those institutions and academic programs that have developed interdependent educational outcomes between formal classroom learning and student's out-of-class experiences the impact is much greater and longer lasting. For those institutions and programs who want to improve this relationship and their overall productivity, this report will help in focusing the conversations.

Jonathan D. Fife
Series Editor, Professor of Higher Education Administration, and
Director, ERIC Clearinghouse on Higher Education

---
[c]*Involving Colleges: Successful Approaches to Fostering Student Learning and Development Outside the Classroom.* San Fransisco: Jossey-Bass.
[d]ASHE-ERIC Higher Education Report No. 6. Washington, D.C.: Association for the Study of Higher Education; ERIC Clearinghouse on Higher Education; GeorgeWashington University, School of Education and Human Development. ED 356 702. 110pp. MF–01; PC–05.

ACKNOWLEDGMENTS

In preparing this report we incurred numerous intellectual and production debts. We are greatly obliged to the many scholars whose research and writing made it possible for us to discern the important contributions that out-of-class experiences make to the goals of higher education. We also wish to thank the many dozens of colleagues around the country who offered practical examples of educationally purposeful out-of-class experiences in response to our presentations during the past few years at meetings of the American Association for Higher Education, the American College Personnel Association, the American Educational Research Association, the Association for the Study of Higher Education, the National Association of Student Personnel Administrators, and the Methodist Board of Higher Education, as well as at institution-based gatherings (e.g., Butler University, California State University–Fresno, Earlham College, Eastern Connecticut State University, Ithaca College, James Madison University, Monroe Community College, Portland State University, University of Minnesota at Morris, University of Iowa, University of Vermont, University of Western Ontario, Wake Forest University). In addition, we are grateful to three anonymous reviewers who suggested ways to improve the presentation. As usual, the ERIC Clearinghouse on Higher Education staff, especially Jon Fife, were helpful, supportive, and responsive.

Working and studying at Indiana University (IU) is a privilege. Our hunt for bibliographic materials, fugitive documents, clear thinking, and colleagueship was successful in large part because IU is both a congenial work environment and rich in academic resources. One of those resources is Joyce Regester, administrative assistant in the School of Education's Department of Educational Leadership and Policy Studies. Joyce knows more than the four of us combined about word processing (and many other things!) and helped us to access and efficiently exchange material electronically. She also produced the figures of the mental models that appear in the Implications section. The outline for these models emerged during a discussion in the Student Learning Project Work Group, a handful of scholars and student affairs practitioners charged by the National Association of Student Personnel Administrators to provide conceptual leadership in seeking ways to more closely connect out-of-class experiences with an institution's academic goals.

Finally, we dedicate this report to those faculty, academic administrators, student life staff, and students who transcend the arbitrary boundaries between in-class and out-of-class settings to create seamless learning environments at their institutions. They know that in the final analysis the measure of institutional productivity that is most important is student learning. Moreover, they recognize that learning and personal development are products of powerful, mutual shaping in-class and out-of-class experiences, academic and social encounters, and faculty- or staff-inspired and peer-induced insights. We trust they will find that our views affirm their vision and that they will be able to use the report to persuade others of the value of trying to better integrate out-of-class experiences with curricular goals.

George D. Kuh, Bloomington, Indiana
Katie Branch Douglas, Bloomington, Indiana
Jon P. Lund, Decorah, Iowa
Jackie Ramin-Gyurnek, Bloomington, Indiana

WARRANT, PURPOSE, AND OVERVIEW

Global competition and demographic, economic, and tech-nological changes make postsecondary education more important than ever. According to pollster Daniel Yankelovich (in Edgerton 1993), 88 percent of U.S. adults agree that a high school diploma is no longer enough to qualify for a well-paying job. Seventy-three percent indicated that a college degree is very important for getting a good job or advancing in one's career. More people than ever want their children or family members to go to college. But they are also increasingly concerned with the cost of higher education and more vocal about what they want and expect for their money (Edgerton 1993).

The same external conditions that make higher education more important also are making colleges and universities more difficult to manage effectively and efficiently. The most significant force is economic. About 40 percent of U.S. edu-cational spending goes to higher education, substantially more than in other countries (House 1994). Most of this support comes from state governments, which over the past decade have reduced funds designated for higher education by more than one quarter, from 19 percent to 14 percent. By 1991–92 state expenditures for education were not keeping up with inflation neither were those of local support (Education Commission of the States 1994). State-assisted institutions have been especially hard hit by declining state appropriations, particularly in those states suffering from weak economies. Penn State and the University of Michigan now receive less than 15 percent of their operating funds from state appropriations. In 1995–96, state support for the University of Oregon is expected to be about 8 percent. This is similar to the decreases in financial support that have occurred in K–12 education during the past two decades.

The inability of state governments to increase support for state-assisted colleges and universities is in part a function of the federal government passing on costs to the state. As a result, 80 to 85 percent of state budgets are earmarked for entitlements, court-ordered elementary school funding, and required state-level matching for increasingly expensive federal programs such as Medicaid (Ewell 1994). In many states, other needs are more pressing--repairing highways, building prisons, and maintaining social services. When scarce discretionary funds are available, elementary and secondary education receive a greater proportion of the budget than does higher education. No one expects these priorities to change in the near future. As a result, higher education in many states has become the budget balancer—the major piece of discretionary spending remaining after mandatory expenditure needs have been addressed (Ewell 1994).

Decreased federal funding for financial aid means that institutions must use more of their own resources to help students. Budget shortfalls also have forced institutions to reduce the number of full-time faculty in the classroom. In some instances this means that fewer students can get the classes they need to graduate in a four- or even five-year period, such as was the case in the California State University system (Goldwhite 1994).

Coupled with the decrease in federal and state funding for higher education are increased demands for institutional accountability. People want evidence that higher education makes a difference (Education Commission of the States 1994; Johnstone 1993; Wingspread Group 1993). State legislatures are considering bills that determine teaching loads and mandate reports on student performance (Edgerton 1993). Regional accrediting associations require outcome measures as evidence of institutional effectiveness.

Further complicating matters at many institutions is the changing nature of student characteristics. At all but a small number of selective, residential institutions, students are different in almost every way from their counterparts of two and three decades ago. Proportionately fewer students are 18 to 23 years old and have traditional academic preparations, more attend college part-time, and many are continuing interrupted educations. Whatever reasons students went to college in the past, the vast majority today seek a credential that qualifies them for a good job in the global economic marketplace (National Association of Student Personnel Administrators 1995).

Enhancing Institutional Productivity
Higher education is facing a challenge similar to that of most American enterprises. Simply put, there is not enough money to support all the things colleges and universities want to do. As a result, higher education must be significantly reduced in size and cost ("To Dance with Change" 1994) by making "major changes—analogous to the restructuring that

is occurring in the corporate and governmental sectors—to control costs and protect quality" (Callan 1995, p. iii). Thus, colleges and universities must become more productive by making better use of existing resources so that students learn more without institutions spending more (Wingspread Group 1993), what Johnstone (1993) called enhancing institutional productivity.

In response to these pressures, many institutions are reallocating resources. These reallocations are redefining the curriculum, faculty roles, and student affairs. Restructuring typically involves reviewing the institution's mission, values, and programs. For example, 71 percent of the institutions participating in the 1994 Campus Trends survey (El-Khawas 1994) had reviewed the missions of academic units during the preceding academic year. Another 16 percent reported they were discussing the possibility of reviewing their mission and revising core activities. Sixty percent of institutions reorganized academic units and 40 percent eliminated academic programs. More than half of the institutions (53 percent) had reorganized student services; about 21 percent had reduced student services staff (El-Khawas 1994).

With regard to undergraduate education, the key restructuring questions are: (1) what factors inhibit and contribute to improved learning productivity and (2) what can be done about them (Johnstone 1993)? Institutional affluence does not seem to be a critical factor. Across a wide array of educational outcomes (e.g., verbal, quantitative, and subject-matter competence; cognitive complexity and intellectual skills; psycho-social traits, attitudes, and values) only trivial relationships exist between traditional measures of institutional quality (e.g., educational expenditures per student, student-faculty ratios, faculty salaries, library holdings, prestige rankings) and net gains, where net gains represent the degree of change attributable to institutional characteristics after taking into account the kinds of students who enroll (Pascarella and Terenzini 1991). Stated another way, "*Real* quality in undergraduate education resides more in an institution's educational climate and what it does programmatically than in its stock of human, financial, and educational resources" (Terenzini and Pascarella 1994, p. 29).

Some institutions have embraced the Wingspread Group's (1993) challenge to put learning first. For example, Syracuse University adopted "to promote learning" as its unifying

...colleges and universities must become more productive by making better use of existing resources so that students learn more without institutions spending more...

theme for integrating the teaching, research, and service functions. Implicit in this focus on learning is a major shift away from the experts (e.g., faculty) who deliver education to students to expecting students themselves to take more responsibility for, and become more actively engaged in, their own learning. Putting learning first focuses attention on

> *the student whose learning is promoted through educa-tion, to the members of our disciplines whose learning is promoted through our published research, into the society at large whose learning is promoted by our teaching, writ-ing, creative activity and professional consulting* (Vincow 1993, p. 2).

One way to increase undergraduate student learning is to make time spent in classes more productive. This can be accomplished by paying greater attention to how, and how well, students learn and to how effectively teachers teach (Angelo and Cross 1993). Another way to increase instruc-tional productivity is to increase class size, which assumes that quality will not suffer under such circumstances (Johnstone 1993). However, suggesting such an approach typically elicits a defensive response from faculty and aca-demic leaders (Benjamin 1993). Moreover, as Johnstone (1993) noted, "While there clearly are faculty and staff at any institution who we wish were harder working, more effec-tive, or just luckier, the popular image of widespread shirk-ing or misplaced priorities is simply wrong (p. 4).

Increased teaching loads and larger class sizes cannot by themselves meet the institutional productivity challenge (Johnstone 1993). Instead, colleges and universities must find ways to encourage students to put forth more effort that will result in gains in learning and personal development that are congruent with the institution's mission and the students' educational and vocational objectives. That is, gains will not come about through more productive teaching necessarily but in more productive learning, including reducing the time that students spend on activities that are not associated with learning (e.g., watching TV, playing cards, napping).

One approach to enhancing learning productivity is to motivate, inspire, and teach students how to assume more responsibility in the educational process. Students cannot be passive: they must become active learners. In its clarion call for reform in higher education, the Wingspread Group (1993) called on institutions to improve the quality of their programs and services by setting higher expectations for student performance:

> *A disturbing and dangerous mismatch exists between what American society needs of higher education and what it is receiving. Nowhere is the mismatch more dangerous than in the quality of undergraduate preparation. . . . Establishing higher expectations, however, will require that students and parents rethink what too many seem to want from education: the credential without the content, the degree without the knowledge and effort it implies* (p. 1).
>
> *Students, at any level of education are the workers in the educational process. They have a major obligation for their own success. Too many students do not behave as though that were the case, apparently believing (as do many parents) that grades are more important for success in life than acquired knowledge, the ability to learn throughout a lifetime, and hard work on campus* (p. 16).

The largest discretionary block of time for most students is outside the classroom. This is true even for part-time students, those with families, and those who work 20 or more hours a week. Thus, another approach to increasing learning productivity is to get more students to take greater advantage of the resources for learning beyond the classroom in which institutions have already invested substantially. These resources are both human (e.g., informal interactions with faculty and staff, librarians, and motivated peers) and physical (e.g., libraries, laboratories, residence halls, and unions).

The idea of getting students to devote more of their out-of-class time to educationally purposeful activities has been around for a while. In the past decade, many scholars have pointed to the importance of these out-of-class experiences to attaining the goals of higher education (Astin 1993b; Baxter Magolda 1992b; Boyer 1987; Chickering and Reisser 1993; Kuh, Schuh, Whitt, and Associates 1991; Kuh 1993a; Pace 1990; Pascarella and Terenzini 1991). Employers also have expressed indirectly an interest in what students gain from their experiences outside the classroom, saying that while students are well-prepared in their major field many

lack the practical competencies needed to be successful in the workplace, what Bruffee (1993) called "the craft of interdependence" (p. 1). These competencies include skills in communication, group process, team work, decision making, and understanding and demonstrating sensitivity to workplace culture (Cappelli 1992; Ewell 1994; Frisz 1984). Although practical competencies can be obtained in classrooms, laboratories, and studios, the nature of many out-of-class activities requires that students become competent in these areas (Kuh 1995). This is because many experiences outside the classroom put the student at the center of learning (Baxter Magolda 1994), demanding that students examine and test their skills and values in a variety of situations not unlike those they will encounter after college. College graduates must be well-educated, learned, and competent, prepared to contribute to and thrive in the complex world in which they will live and work.

> *Society's needs will be well served if colleges and universities wholeheartedly commit themselves to providing students with opportunities to experience and reflect on the world beyond the campus. Books and lectures provide an intellectual grounding in the realities of the marketplace and of the nation's social dilemmas. But there is no substitute for experience. Academic work should be complemented by the kinds of knowledge derived from first-hand experience, such as contributing to the well-being of others, participating in political campaigns, and working with the enterprises that create wealth in our society* (Wingspread Group 1993, p. 10).

However, many faculty members as well as academic and student affairs administrators do not direct their energies to cultivating the natural links between what students learn in their classes to their lives outside the classroom. That is, their behavior seems to reflect the erroneous belief that whatever is worth learning can only be learned in the classroom, thus creating debilitating psychological and symbolic boundaries between the formal curriculum and other learning and personal development experiences.

In summary, many factors are forcing institutions to become more productive. Increasingly diverse students must be prepared to work in a global economy that requires complex job skills (Tucker 1995). However, many of these students are not prepared for college-level work, lacking the academic and social skills needed to take advantage of the resources for learning and personal development colleges offer. Moreover, it is no longer sufficient to prepare a student in a single discipline and assume that preparation will be sufficient for a lifetime of work.

No single experience, or category of experiences, are precursors of the desired changes in knowledge, skills, and attitudes that occur during college. Rather, these changes appear to result from a set of cumulative, interrelated, and mutually supporting experiences sustained over an extended period of time (Terenzini and Pascarella 1994). In other words, students change as whole, integrated persons; virtually all their academic, nonacademic, in-class, and out-of-class experiences are potentially important to these changes. What seems to be key is the breadth, as well as depth, of student involvement in both the intellectual and social experiences of college. That is, most important is a student's total level of campus engagement, especially when the academic, interpersonal, and out-of-class experiences are mutually supporting and relevant to a particular educational outcome. Out-of-class activities (e.g., child-rearing, work, community service, leadership in organizations) are potentially powerful adjuncts to the formal academic program when students apply what they are learning in the classroom to these settings and vice versa (i.e., using their out-of-class experiences to make meaning of what they are studying in class).

This suggests that the tighter the connections between the curriculum and students' out-of-class lives, the greater the benefits. To motivate students to use their out-of-class time more wisely, faculty, academic administrators, and student affairs personnel must themselves behave in ways that transcend the artificial boundaries between in-class and out-of-class learning experiences. To support such a culture change, a compelling case based on evidence is needed.

Purpose
Out-of-class experiences tend to be overlooked when estimating the effects of college attendance and how to enhance student learning. Therefore, it is important that the contribu-

tions of these experiences in attaining the purposes of under-graduate education be identified so that they can be addressed intentionally in efforts to promote student learning.

The purpose of this report is to summarize what is known about student learning outside the classroom and to suggest ideas for how to connect academic goals and class-room experiences to students' lives outside the classroom and vice-versa. The thesis on which the report is based is that if institutions could get students to use their out-of-class time in more educationally purposeful ways, and more closely link the curriculum and students' classroom experiences with what students do with their lives outside the classroom, levels of undergraduate learning will increase thereby boosting institutional productivity.

Apportioning what students learn during college into discrete categories of in-class and out-of-class experiences does violence to the assumption of holistic talent development (Astin 1985) and the empirical research on the impact of college on students (Pascarella and Terenzini 1991), which indicates that what students do outside the classroom influences what they do in class and vice versa.

> *The concepts of "learning," "personal development," and "student development" are inextricably intertwined . . . inseparable. [Even though] colleges traditionally organize their activities into "academic affairs" ("learning" . . . "cognitive development") and "student affairs" ("affective" or "personal development") . . . this dichotomy has little relevance to post-college life, where . . . one's job performance, family life, and community activities are all highly dependent on cognitive and affective skills. Indeed . . . many important adult skills (e.g., leadership, creativity, citizenship, ethical behavior . . .) are both cognitive and affective. [And] research shows that the impact of an institution's "academic" program is mediated by what happens outside the classroom* (American College Personnel Association 1994, p. 1).

Moreover, the combination of experiences inside and out-side the classroom makes unique contributions to student learning and personal development while in-class and out-of-class experiences make their own independent contributions. Thus, ignoring out-of-class experiences and their

impact on desired outcomes of higher education is
foolhardy and shortsighted.

Overview and Scope
The report is organized around three questions:

1. How do out-of-class experiences of undergraduates contribute to the goals of higher education (Bowen 1977)
   and valued outcomes of college (Pascarella and Terenzini
   1991)?
2. What are the institutional conditions (e.g., policies, programs, practices) that encourage students to use institutional resources and their out-of-class time in more
   educationally purposeful ways?
3. What can academic administrators, faculty, student affairs
   staff, students, and others do to create richer, more
   engaging environments that connect out-of-class experiences (including opportunities beyond the boundaries of
   the campus) with the institution's academic purposes?

Out-of-class experiences are broadly defined to include
all activities in which students engage during undergraduate
study that are either directly or indirectly related to their
learning and performance and occur beyond the formal
classroom, studio, or laboratory setting. Such activities
include, but are not limited to, studying in the library, interacting with peers and faculty, participating in organized
campus-based events (e.g., orientation, cultural and theatrical performances) and activities (e.g., organizations), working on or off the campus, and using other resources colleges
provide for undergraduate learning and personal development, whether human (instructors, advisers, coaches, administrators) or physical (libraries, laboratories, studios, unions,
playing fields, residences). Such experiences are educationally purposeful when they are congruent with the institution's educational purposes and a student's own educational
aspirations (Kuh et al. 1991).
   We first describe the approach used to identify the relevant literature and the outcomes framework used to analyze
the pertinent research. The link between involvement in out-
of-class activities and educational attainment is examined
next. Then, the out-of-class experiences associated with
persistence and various categories of outcomes are

discussed. From the literature we distilled nine conditions that characterize developmentally powerful out-of-class environments. Such environments encourage students to take advantage of learning opportunities both in and outside the classroom. Moreover, taken together these conditions encourage students to integrate what they are learning through their out-of-class experiences to their academic studies, and vice versa. The report concludes with implications for those interested in encouraging the use of out-of-class time in more productive, educationally purposeful ways—governing board members, presidents, academic administrators, student affairs administrators, faculty, and students.

WHAT THE LITERATURE SAYS ABOUT LIFE OUTSIDE THE CLASSROOM AND DESIRED OUTCOMES OF COLLEGE

Pascarella and Terenzini (1991) reviewed the college outcomes literature through about 1990. However, the outcomes associated with out-of-class activities are not readily identifiable from their excellent, massive synthesis. In addition, some since-published studies have addressed the links between out-of-class experiences and outcomes. To distill the contributions of out-of-class experiences of undergraduates to valued educational goals, three bodies of literature were reviewed:

1. Multiple institution studies of student learning and personal development such as Astin's (1993b) longitudinal study of 25,000 undergraduate students from 217 four-year colleges and universities conducted under the auspices of the Cooperative Institutional Research Program (CIRP) and Pace's (1990) analysis of College Student Experience Questionnaire (CSEQ) data from several hundred institutions;
2. Syntheses of extant research (e.g., Bowen 1977; Feldman and Newcomb 1969), drawing extensively on the material in Pascarella and Terenzini's (1991) comprehensive review of college outcomes focused specifically on the contributions of out-of-class experiences to valued outcomes of college; and
3. More recently published studies not reviewed by Pascarella and Terenzini (e.g., Baxter Magolda 1992b; Chickering and Reisser 1993; King and Kitchener 1994; Kuh 1993a 1995), including those from the National Study of Student Learning, a research track funded through the National Center on Postsecondary Teaching, Learning and Assessment (e.g., Nora, Hagedorn, Cabrera, and Pascarella 1994; Pascarella, Bohr, Nora, Zusman, Inman, and Desler 1993; Pascarella, Terenzini, and Blimling 1994; Pascarella, Edison, Nora, Hagedorn, and Terenzini In press; Pascarella, Edison, Whitt, Nora, Hagedorn, and Terenzini In press; Springer, Terenzini, Pascarella, and Nora 1995; Terenzini, Springer, Pascarella, and Nora 1995).

A fourth literature was consulted, learning theory and research in the tradition of cognitive and developmental psychology (e.g., Alexander and Murphy 1994; Bandura 1977 1986; Renninger, Hidi, and Krapp 1992; Vera and

Simon 1993), to distill implications for ways to make out-of-class activities more educationally purposeful.

Guiding Frameworks

Two analytical frameworks are used to interpret the findings: (a) the involvement principle, and (b) person-environment interaction frameworks. The involvement principle posits that the more time and energy students expend in educationally purposeful activities, the more they benefit (e.g., Astin 1984; Kuh 1981; Pace 1979; The Study Group 1984). Astin's (1984) five postulates of involvement illustrate why time and energy are important to learning:

1. Involvement is the investment of physical and psychological energy in various activities. The activities may be quite general (e.g., the freshman year) or specific (e.g., preparing for a chemistry examination);
2. Involvement occurs along a continuum, in that different students exhibit different degrees of involvement in a given activity or task with the same student manifesting different degrees of involvement in different activities at different times;
3. Involvement has both quantitative and qualitative features. The extent of a student's involvement in academic work, for instance, can be measured quantitatively (e.g., hours devoted to studying) and qualitatively (e.g., whether the student reviews and comprehends reading assignments or simply stares at the textbook and daydreams);
4. The amount of educational benefit associated with any activity is directly proportional to the quality and quantity of a student's investment of time and energy; and
5. The effectiveness of any educational policy or practice is directly related to the capacity of that policy or practice to increase student involvement.

Person-environment interaction frameworks (e.g., Baird 1988; Huebner 1989; Lewin 1936; Pervin 1968; Stern 1970) are broadly defined to include social ecology and campus culture (Kuh and Whitt 1988). Taken together, these views indicate that mutual shaping occurs between individuals and their environments. Thus, under certain conditions, it is possible to influence the outcomes associated with college attendance.

Our analysis of the literature also was guided by the following assumptions (American College Personnel Association 1994):

1. Talent development (Astin 1985) is the over-arching goal of undergraduate education;
2. The domains of learning and personal development are inextricably intertwined and overlap in some areas; each affects the other in myriad ways;
3. Both students and institutions contribute to student learning; that is, learning and personal development occur through transactions between students and their environments; and
4. Experiences in various in-class and out-of-class settings, both on and off the campus, contribute to learning and personal development.

Educational Attainment
In this section we summarize the literature related to out-of-class experiences, persistence, and degree attainment (table 1). Educational attainment (i.e., obtaining one's desired educational objective) is not a behavioral or psychological outcome (Astin 1977) as are the other outcomes domains discussed later. Nevertheless, persistence is important because the closer students come to attaining their educational objectives, the greater their learning and personal development gains (Pascarella and Terenzini 1991). For this reason, it is important to understand the relationships between out-of-class experiences, persistence, and degree attainment. For example, the more satisfied a student is with the institution, choice of major, friends, academic progress and so forth, the more likely that student is to graduate (Tinto 1993) and more fully realize the benefits of a college education.

In general, many out-of-class experiences are positively related to student persistence and, therefore, attainment of students' educational objectives. The findings from this research can be divided into five categories: (a) general institutional characteristics; (b) specific institutional subenvironments; (c) student satisfaction; (d) social and academic integration; and (e) student support services.

In general, many out-of-class experiences are positively related to student persistence and, therefore, attainment of students' educational objectives.

TABLE 1

OUT-OF CLASS ACTIVITIES ASSOCIATED WITH PERSISTENCE AND EDUCATIONAL ATTAINMENT

Variables	Impact
General Institutional Characteristics	
Institutional size	Mixed[a]
Attending a historically black institution for African American students	Positive
Attending a women's college for women	Positive
Institutional Subenvironments	
Living on campus	Positive
Fraternity or sorority membership	Positive
Working part-time on campus	Positive
Student Satisfaction	
Student-faculty interaction	Positive
Student-student interaction	Positive
Institutional emphasis on diversity	Positive
Absence of perceived sense of community	Negative
Working off-campus	Negative
Social and Academic Integration	
Participating in orientation	Positive
Participating in extra-curricular activities	Positive
Interaction with faculty outside the classroom	Positive
Quality of relations with peers	Positive
Living in campus residence	Positive
Student Support Services	
New student orientation	Positive
Low ratio of student affairs staff to students	Positive
Advising programs	Mixed[a]

[a]The research is contradictory in this area; that is, some studies show that the activity is positively related to persistence, other studies indicate the activity is negatively related.

General institutional characteristics

Certain aspects of an institution's out-of-class environments are either directly or indirectly related to the attainment of educational goals. Among the more important seem to be institutional size and racial or gender composition.

The effects of institutional size on persistence and degree attainment are inconsistent and contradictory (Pascarella and Terenzini 1991). For example, Stoecker and Pascarella (1991) found that institutional size was negatively related to involvement in social activities, which consequently affected educational attainment for women (Pascarella and Terenzini 1991). A similar relationship was found between institutional size and the educational attainment of African American and white men and women (Pascarella and Terenzini 1991; Stoecker, Pascarella, and Wolfle 1988). The crucial aspect of size is its effect on students' ability to become integrated socially into the institution. That is, large institutions negatively influence social involvement and integration during college, even after taking into account such characteristics as place of residence and institutional selectivity (Astin 1977; Chickering and Reisser 1993; Stoecker and Pascarella 1991; Stoecker, Pascarella, and Wolfle 1988).

An institution's racial composition appears to have an influence on educational attainment, an effect that may be mediated primarily through social involvement. Many have suggested that African American students find the environments of many predominantly white colleges and universities to be alienating compared with those of historically black institutions (Allen 1987; Blackwell 1981; Edmonds 1984; Livingston and Stewart 1987; Loo and Rolison 1986; Suen 1983). Thus, persistence rates for students of color at predominantly white institutions are often far lower than those for white students. In contrast, African American students attending predominantly black institutions are more likely to persist and attain their educational objective (Astin 1975; Cross and Astin 1981; Pascarella, Smart, Ethington, and Nettles 1987). Studies conducted by Fleming (1984); Nettles, Thoeny, and Gosman (1986); and Willie and Cunnigen (1981) found "that black students who attend predominantly black institutions benefit from a supportive social, cultural, and racial environment that enhances their successful adaptation to the academic demands of undergraduate life" (Pascarella and Terenzini 1991, p. 382). However, Gurin and Epps (1975) studying first-year African American students from nine historically black institutions found no significant relationships between the degree of involvement on campus and educational aspirations, after controlling for institutional selectivity and initial aspirations. In any event, the effect of historically black colleges and universities on African American students' attainment seems to be small, estimated at less than 1 percent of the total variance in educational attainment (Pascarella and Terenzini 1991).

Attending a single-sex institution seems to enhance persistence and educational attainment, especially for women (Astin 1977 1993b; El-Khawas 1980; Tidball and Kistiakowsky 1976). This effect is, in part, a function of the supportive intellectual and social climate where women perform all the intellectual and social leadership tasks and are exposed to appropriate role models (Monteiro 1980; Smith 1988; Tidball 1980 1986). As with racial composition, the total effect of gender composition on educational attainment appears to be small, accounting for less than 1 percent of the total variance (Pascarella and Terenzini 1991).

Finally, students who adhere to a particular religious faith and attend institutions affiliated with that faith have a stronger commitment to their institution and to persisting and accomplishing their educational objectives (Astin 1975; Clewell and Ficklen 1986).

Specific institutional subenvironments
Certain subenvironments (e.g., residence halls, work settings, student organizations) specific to various institutions or institutional types have been shown to affect persistence and educational attainment.

Living environments. After examining persistence of African American and other first-year students at a regional public university, Thompson, Samiratedu, and Rafter (1993) determined that academic progress and retention were significantly higher for those students who lived on campus compared with those who lived off campus, irrespective of race, gender, or admissions status (i.e., regular admission or those who did not meet the standard requirements). Membership in fraternities or sororities also has positive effects on persistence and degree completion (Astin 1975).

However, students who live on campus typically differ from their counterparts who do not (e.g., higher family socioeconomic status, aptitude, and aspirations) which make these students more likely to persist and graduate than their counterparts who commute to campus (Astin 1985; Chickering 1974; Pascarella 1984). These initial differences are accentuated by living on campus. Nevertheless, the effect of the residential nature of colleges on persistence and accomplishment of educational objectives is small, accounting for perhaps no more than 1 percent of the total variance (Pascarella and Terenzini 1991). In addition, the effect of the residential experience seems to have differential impact based on institutional characteristics. For example, the effect of living on campus had its greatest impact on degree attainment of first-year students at four-year colleges and a smaller positive effect on students at four-year universities; the effect was trivial for students at two-year colleges (Astin 1973). The latter result may be flawed, however, due to the smaller number of two-year institutions with residence facilities (Pascarella and Terenzini 1991).

The context of the living environment also is important in that some living experiences are richer and more developmentally powerful, thus influencing persistence and degree attainment to varying degrees. What seems to be important, then, for maximizing the developmental impact of the living unit is to emphasize factors such as formal policies and a peer culture that value academic achievement as well as social integration (Pascarella and Terenzini 1991).

Work. Part-time employment on campus, persistence, and degree attainment are positively correlated (Astin 1982; Ehrenberg and Sherman 1987). However, off-campus employment is negatively related to educational attainment (Astin 1982; Ehrenberg and Sherman 1987).

Involvement in activities. Participation in cocurricular activities is positively related to persistence (Carroll 1988; Mallinckrodt 1988; Mallinckrodt and Sedlacek 1987; Nelson, Scott, and Bryan 1984; Simpson, Baker, and Mellinger 1980). Hanks and Eckland (1976) speculated that involvement in cocurricular activities may influence persistence in two ways: (a) students are connected psychologically and socially to an affinity group that is achievement-oriented, which reinforces the desire to graduate, and (b) students become involved in activities that allow them to acquire skills and competencies that make it more likely they can succeed in college (e.g., interpersonal skills, self-confidence) (Pascarella and Terenzini 1991). After examining CIRP data, Ethington (1994) concluded that students who were more involved had significantly higher levels of educational attainment. Ethington also found that "differences in educational attainment levels

of students [was] to a far greater extent the result of individual differences than it [was] differences in the types of institutions they attend" (p. 11).

The extent to which participation in cocurricular activities affects persistence seems to be conditional in that such participation influences students differently. Pascarella and Chapman (1983) and Pascarella and Terenzini (1979) found that involvement had the greatest positive impact on persistence for students with lower levels of commitment to the institution and their educational goals; that is, the greater the commitment to attaining educational goals, the less important engagement in campus life is to persistence. Pascarella and Terenzini (1983) and Ethington and Smart (1986) found that involvement had a greater positive effect on first-year persistence for women than for men. Because a variety of out-of-class experiences seem to be related to student commitment to the institutions (e.g., involvement in athletics, fraternity or sorority membership), there seems to be a link between participation in certain out-of-class activities and persistence via increased student commitment to the institution and to earning a degree.

Student satisfaction

Student satisfaction with the institution is an important but sometimes overlooked variable in determining the quality of the undergraduate experience. Satisfaction represents a sense that the student feels he or she belongs at, and is loyal to, the institution (Lenning, Beal, and Sauer 1980; Tinto 1987) and is highly correlated with involvement (Abrahamowicz 1988; Astin 1993b; Holland and Huba 1991; Russel and Skinkle 1990; Whitt 1994), persistence (Pascarella and Terenzini 1991; Tinto 1987), and academic performance (Bean 1980; Bean and Bradley 1986; Bean and Vesper 1994; Pike 1991 1993).

> *Although an affective measure, it may be argued that student satisfaction is one of the most direct tests of post-secondary success. . . . Given that individual students are the primary beneficiaries of the college experience, asking them how satisfied they are with those experiences is an obvious way to measure this success* (Gielow and Lee, cited in Knox, Lindsay, and Kolb 1992, pp. 305–06).

Moreover, "the student's degree of satisfaction with the college experience proves to be much less dependent on entering characteristics . . . and more susceptible to influence from the college environment" (Astin 1993b, p. 277). Thus, satisfaction with the college experience is a factor that warrants attention by institutional agents (Astin 1977 1993b; Bean and Vesper 1994; Knox, Lindsay, and Kolb 1992).

A number of out-of-class experiences have been linked to satisfaction. In perhaps the most extensive investigation of environmental factors associated with satisfaction, Astin (1993b) found that satisfaction with the total college experience was positively associated with greater student-faculty and frequent student-student interaction, leaving home to attend college, and the institution's emphasis on diversity. Satisfaction with the overall college experience was negatively affected by the absence of a perceived sense of community and working off campus. Astin (1993b) also found that satisfaction with student support services was positively related to the percentage of expenditures devoted to these services.

Student satisfaction seems to have a stronger effect on grades than vice versa (Bean and Bradley 1986). Moreover, faculty-student interaction and peer interaction seems to positively influence satisfaction (Astin 1993b; Bean and Kuh 1984) while attending cultural events (plays, films, concerts) has been found to be negatively related (Pike 1991).

Using data from the 1979 follow-up to the *National Longitudinal Study of the High School Class of 1972* (NLS-72), Knox, Lindsay, and Kolb (1992) found weak, direct effects of some out-of-class variables on satisfaction. For example, students at larger institutions tend to be more satisfied with recreation and sports facilities. Also, students at residential campuses report higher levels of satisfaction with social life. It may be, though, that the latter relationship is in part an artifact of institutional prestige (i.e., residential institutions tend to be perceived as more prestigious).

In a study of first- and second-year honors students, Bean and Vesper (1994) found that for both men and women satisfaction was positively related with confidence in academic abilities and perceiving their courses to be relevant. Having friends, contact with adviser, and living on campus contributed to satisfaction for women. This finding supports the research of Gilligan (1982) and Belenky, Clinchy, Goldberg, and Tarule (1986), which suggests that women respond positively to environments that emphasize relational qualities. In contrast, for men, major and career certainty were significant factors.

Using the College Student Satisfaction Questionnaire (CSSQ), Robertson (1980) found no statistical differences in student satisfaction with respect to the social life or physical conditions of the environment between African American and white students at a predominantly white institution in the South.

Finally, in a study of the relationship between serving as an orientation assistant and satisfaction, Holland and Huba (1991) found statistically significant differences in satisfaction between those who did (more satisfied) and those who did not (less satisfied) have this experience.

Social and academic integration
Social integration is often measured as a composite of peer-peer interactions and faculty-student interactions while academic integration reflects satisfaction with academic progress and choice of major. Orientation programs, for example, have a positive impact on persistence through encouraging students to become integrated into the institution's academic and social systems (Pascarella and Terenzini 1991).

Grosset (1991) examined persistence of "younger" (age 23 and younger) and "older" (more than 23 years old) students using components of Tinto's (1975) theoretical model of student attrition. Two variables discriminated between younger persisters and nonpersisters: academic integration variables related to out-of-class interactions with faculty and the amount of cognitive progress reported by students. Discriminating between older persisters and nonpersisters were self-assessments of study skills and cognitive progress. The quality of the academic experience, particularly out-of-class contact with faculty, seemed to be the most influential factor for younger students; social integration was also important but to a lesser degree. Older students' perceptions of their readiness for college-level academic work was the most important factor in persistence. Brower (1992) found that student persistence was significantly higher for those students who focused less on making friends and time management issues during the first semester.

After examining students' academic and social integration at community colleges and their intent to graduate from a four-year school, Bers and Smith (1991) concluded that those factors influencing persistence for four-year students also held for community college students. The variables discriminating between persisters and nonpersisters were intent to re-enroll, educational objectives, precollege characteristics, and employment status; academic integration and social integration discriminated between the two groups to a lesser degree.

Peers are particularly important with regard to social integration because students are more likely to stay in school when they feel comfortable and connected to other students with similar interests and aspirations (social integration) (Bean 1980; Spady 1970; Tinto 1975 1987). For this reason, perhaps, fraternity and sorority membership are positively related to persistence (Astin 1975). In addition, institutions with higher levels of student social interaction also have higher levels of student educational aspirations (Pascarella 1985). Cooperative Institutional Research Program data (Astin 1977 1982 1993b) indicate that

> *obtaining the bachelor's degree was positively influenced by attending a college with a high level of cohesion in the peer environment (the number of peers whom the student regarded as close friends) or where students frequently participated in college-sponsored activities and there was a high level of personal involvement with and concern for the individual student* (Pascarella and Terenzini 1991, p. 384).

However, Gurin and Epps (1975), studying African American first-year students at nine historically black institutions, found no significant relationship between the degree of student interaction on campus and students' educational aspirations.

The research on the relationships between faculty-student interactions outside the classroom and persistence and degree attainment is generally favorable, though somewhat mixed (Pascarella 1980). Some (Astin 1977 1993b; Pascarella

SAINT PETER'S COLLEGE LIBRARY
JERSEY CITY, NEW JERSEY 07306

and Terenzini 1976 1977; Terenzini and Pascarella 1980) have found persistence to be "positively and significantly related to total amount of student-faculty non-classroom contact with faculty and particularly to frequency of interactions with faculty to discuss intellectual matters" (Pascarella and Terenzini 1991, p. 394). However, others (Bean 1980 1985; Voorhees 1987) concluded that student-faculty informal contact was unrelated to persistence. Because most of these studies were conducted at single-institutions, the contradictory findings probably reflect institutional differences, meaning that the benefits of student-faculty interaction vary, depending on the student and the institution (Pascarella and Terenzini 1991).

However, faculty-student social interactions seem to positively influence educational aspirations (Gurin and Epps 1975; Hearn 1987; Pascarella 1985) and degree completion (Pascarella, Smart, and Ethington 1986; Stoecker, Pascarella, and Wolfle 1988). Although the reason for this relationship is not clear, it seems likely that when faculty engage students outside the classroom, and these interactions are positive, that students may feel affirmed and develop a stronger bond with the institution through the relationship. These interactions may reinforce a student's initial goals and deepen the commitment to graduate (Pascarella and Terenzini 1991).

Christie and Dinham (1991) used open-ended interviews to explore the factors associated with persistence for a small group of students at a large research university. Two types of institutional experiences were most salient in terms of social integration: living in campus residence halls and participating in cocurricular activities. These experiences provide opportunities for students to become involved in cocurricular activities and to meet other students, thus providing access to campus-based social networks which reduces the amount of contact with friends from high school.

For this reason, at commuter institutions there seems to be little relationship between persistence and social integration (i.e., interaction with faculty and peers and participation in extracurricular activities) (Braxton and Brier 1989; Pascarella and Chapman 1983; Pascarella, Duby, Terenzini,and Iverson 1983; Pascarella and Terenzini 1991; Williamson and Creamer 1988). An exception is Nora and Rendon's (1990) study of community college students (three fourths of whom were Hispanic) where social integration had a significant positive effect on students' predisposition to transfer. Perhaps students who have the support of peers, faculty, and family are more likely to have a positive view toward transferring to another institution in order to attain their educational objectives.

Finally, parents and peers seem to influence students' decisions to stay or leave to a greater extent than faculty. This suggests that who students talk with outside of class about their studies and future goals significantly influence persistence (Bank, Slavings, and Biddle 1990).

Student support services

Some evidence suggests that the ratio of student development professionals to students influences persistence. Hedlund and Jones (1970) found that all the two-year colleges in their sample with a ratio of 1 student development professional to 150 students or fewer graduated 50 percent or more of their students in two years contrasted with only 20 percent of the colleges with a ratio of more than 1:150. Astin (1993b) reported a similar relationship between persistence and resources allocated to student services and personnel. Pascarella and Terenzini (1991) cautioned, however, that such findings are confounded by many factors including systematic differences in the ability of students attending certain institutions.

Forrest (1985) controlled for entering student academic ability and found that institutions that provided the most extensive orientation and advising programs had higher graduation rates. Other studies show similar results (Dunphy, Miller, Woodruff, and Nelson 1987; Fidler and Hunter 1989). However, student participation in orientation may only have a trivial, statistically nonsignificant direct effect on persistence after taking into account students' educational aspirations, commitment to graduation, academic aptitude, and socioeconomic status. Orientation also may have a positive effect on persistence through its influence on social integration and subsequent commitment to the institution.

Advising programs, on the other hand, have inconsistent effects on persistence. Several studies found positive effects (Brigman, Kuh, and Stager 1982; Taylor 1982), while others report statistically nonsignificant effects (Aitken 1982; Kowalski 1977). As with orientation, the quality of academic

...parents and peers seem to influence students' decisions to stay or leave to a greater extent than faculty.

advising may also have an indirect effect when factors such as high school grades, gender, age, and so forth are taken into account (Metzner 1989).

In a study evaluating the effects of an office specifically designed to improve persistence through encouraging students to get involved in social and academic activities, Wolfe (1993) found no difference between commuter and resident student persistence. In fact, members from both groups who participated in programs sponsored by the office demonstrated significantly higher withdrawal behaviors during the intervention period compared with students who did not participate. This unexpected finding may be a function of the fact that participants who wished to be more involved socially may have left the institution to seek out an environment that encouraged social behavior, while academic integration may have been a more salient factor for those who persisted.

Outcomes Clusters

In this section, we examine the links between out-of-class experiences and a broad spectrum of desired outcomes of postsecondary education. The typology used to examine the learning and personal development outcomes associated with out-of-class experiences is based on the one developed by Kuh (1993a). The outcomes are organized into five clusters:

1. Cognitive complexity: cognitive skills including reflective thought, critical thinking (e.g., ability to summarize information accurately and perceive logical coherences and discernable themes and patterns across different sources of information), quantitative reasoning, and intellectual flexibility (i.e., openness to new ideas and different points of view);
2. Knowledge acquisition and application: understanding knowledge from a range of disciplines and physical, geographic, economic, political, religious, and cultural realities, and the ability to relate knowledge to daily life including using information presented in one class in other classes or other areas of life;
3. Humanitarianism: an understanding and appreciation of human differences including an increased sensitivity to the needs of others;

4. Interpersonal and intrapersonal competence: a coherent, integrated constellation of personal attributes (e.g., identity, self-esteem, confidence, integrity, appreciation for the aesthetic and spiritual qualities of life and the natural world, sense of civic responsibility) and skills (e.g., how to work with people different from oneself); and
5. Practical competence: skills reflecting an enhanced capacity to manage one's personal affairs (e.g., time management, decision making), to be economically self-sufficient, and to be vocationally competent.

Although the Kuh typology is based exclusively on benefits students attributed to out-of-class experiences, it is similar in scope to those developed by others (Astin 1977 1993b; Bowen 1977; Lenning 1976; Micek, Service, and Lee 1975). In addition, it accounts for all the outcome domains distilled from the literature by Pascarella and Terenzini (1991): knowledge and subject matter competence, cognitive skills and intellectual growth, psychosocial changes, attitudes and values, moral development, educational attainment, career choice and development, economic benefits, and quality of life.

Cognitive complexity
Reviewed in this section are the skills and attitudes associated with out-of-class experiences that enable a college-educated person to think critically and to evaluate logically or assess the quality of one's own thinking and experience by exercising independent judgment (table 2). Some studies have not found links between out-of-class experiences and cognitive development. For example, Hood (1984) found no significant relationships between gains in cognitive complexity and such variables as place of residence, work experience, and participation in various campus activities. The type of out-of-class activity in which a student participates, or the nature of the institutional environment in which the activity occurs (e.g., academic theme-oriented residence, fraternity house) may explain why some studies show significant changes in cognitive complexity while others do not.

When gains in cognitive development are linked to out-of-class experiences, they tend to be related to the amount of effort students expend in educationally purposeful activities, such as studying or talking with peers and faculty about

TABLE 2

OUT-OF-CLASS ACTIVITIES ASSOCIATED WITH GAINS IN COGNITIVE COMPLEXITY

Activity	Impact
Student-faculty interaction	Positive
Living in academic theme residences	Positive
Living in campus residences	Mixed[a]
Working (on or off campus)	None[b]
Balanced engagement in academic and social activities	Positive
Attending a historically black institution for African American students	Positive
Fraternity membership for white men	Negative
Fraternity membership for African American men	Positive
Sorority membership	Negative

[a]The research is contradictory in this area; that is, some studies show that the activity is positively related to gains in cognitive complexity, other studies indicate the activity is negatively related.

[b]Studies indicate neither a positive nor negative relationship between the activity and gains in cognitive complexity.

advising matters (Frost 1991) or other issues related to their studies (e.g., paper topics, graduate school) (Astin 1993b; Pace 1990). For example, studies of seniors (Gaff 1973; Wilson, Wood, and Gaff 1974; Wilson, Gaff, Dienst, Wood, and Bavry 1975) show that those more involved in certain activities (intellectual, vocational, athletic, political, social) made greater progress on dimensions of cognitive growth (learning abstractions, applying principles, evaluating materials and methods) than those who were less involved. Based on interviews with seniors from twelve institutions, Kuh (1995) found that the majority of the out-of-class antecedents of gains in cognitive complexity were distributed across five areas: (a) peer interaction, (b) academic activities (e.g., studying), (c) other miscellaneous antecedents (e.g., influence of family, illness), (d) campus ethos, and (e) leadership responsibilities.

Such findings suggest that student cognitive growth may be influenced by a variety of experiences and conditions on a campus, particularly when out-of-class climates and experiences complement and encourage students to integrate what they learn in class with their lives outside the classroom (Kuh 1995). These activities may be especially important for African American students (MacKay and Kuh 1994) and older, part-time students who seem to benefit more in terms of cognitive development from the amount of time they invest in studying and related activities (Arnold, Kuh, Vesper, and Schuh 1993; Kuh, Vesper and Krehbiel 1994).

Student-faculty contact. A number of studies have found positive correlations between cognitive complexity outcomes and the quality of relations between students and faculty (Endo and Harpel 1983; Pascarella et al. 1983; Terenzini and Pascarella 1980; Volkwein, King, and Terenzini 1986). Wilson et al. (1975) reported that those seniors who spent the most time with faculty outside of class also exhibited the greatest gains in cognitive outcomes (e.g., comprehension, interpretation, evaluation, or extrapolation abilities) (Pascarella and Terenzini 1991). Kuh (1995) reported that only about a quarter of the gains in cognitive complexity were associated with academics and faculty contact with a higher proportion of men linking their contacts with faculty with gains in this area and women more frequently attributing gains to contacts with peers. In general, students reporting greater gains in cognitive development are those who: (a) perceive faculty as being concerned with teaching and student development; (b) have developed a close, influential relationship with at least one faculty member; and (c) report that their peers have had an important influence on their development.

Baxter Magolda (1992b) found that students at advanced, more complex levels of intellectual development (as assessed by the Measure of Epistemological Reflection, an instrument based on Perry's 1970 scheme of intellectual and ethical development) prefer interactions with faculty during which the faculty treat students as partners in constructing knowledge. Students at less complex levels of intellectual development prefer that faculty assume the role of authority by structuring assignments and removing ambiguity and multiple interpretations by identifying right and wrong answers.

Living and work environments. Several researchers have noted relationships between the characteristics of living arrangements and cognitive development. For example,

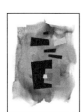

Pascarella and Terenzini (1980) found that first-year students in living-learning residences rated the institutional environment significantly stronger in intellectual press and sense of community and also reported significantly greater gains in cognitive development compared with their counterparts in other campus residences. Living-learning programs also are associated with declines in authoritarian or dogmatic reasoning (Lacy 1978; Newcomb, Brown, Kulik, Reimer, and Revelle 1971; Suczek 1972).

Winter, McClelland, and Stewart (1981) found a statistically significant negative association with gains on the Test of Thematic Analysis (an essay assessment of critical thinking) and student participation in residence hall-sponsored activities. They speculated that campus housing does not necessarily provide an environment conducive to intellectual stimulation because students are insulated from the experiences or activities that challenge comfortable ways of thinking and behaving compared with students who live off campus (see also Blimling 1993).

In a study of commuter students and those living in campus residences, Pascarella et al. (1993) found that students who lived on campus exhibited greater gains in critical thinking than those who commuted. According to Pace (1990), students who lived on campus benefitted more in terms of intellectual development even though their participation in relevant activities as measured by the CSEQ Activity Scales is not much higher than those who live off campus. This suggests that it may not be the activities themselves that promote or foster development, but the contact with peers and others that such activities produce. Pascarella et al. (1993) concluded:

> *Residential living may be most influential in fostering cognitive growth in areas that are not closely linked to specific course or curricular experiences. . . . General cognitive growth during college is fostered not just by course work and academic involvement, but also by social and intellectual interaction with peers and faculty* (p. 219).

Such interactions are more likely to occur when students live on campus than if they commute (Chickering 1974; Pascarella and Terenzini 1991).

With regard to work, no significant differences were found in critical thinking gains for students who worked on campus, worked off campus, or did not work during the first year of college (Pascarella, Bohr, Nora, Desler, and Zusman 1994).

Academic and social involvement. Engagement in both academic and certain types of social activities appear to contribute to intellectual skill development. For example, Pascarella (1984) used the Watson-Glaser Critical Thinking Appraisal to examine the relationships between changes in critical thinking during the first year and a variety of factors (e.g., academic and social experiences, place of residence, time spent studying, cocurricular activities, number of intellectually oriented interactions with faculty and peers). These factors had only trivial and statistically nonsignificant relationships with critical thinking at the end of the first year when the initial level of critical thinking was taken into account. But when the variables were combined to create a composite estimate of student social and intellectual involvement, a statistically significant association was found between involvement and critical thinking at the end of the freshman year. Similarly, Ory and Braskamp (1988) and Pace (1987 1990) found that the level of student involvement or effort in both academic (intellectual) and interpersonal experiences correlated significantly with a measure of intellectual skill development. Fleming (1982 1984) studied groups of first-year students and seniors at a predominantly African American and a predominantly white institution and found greater first year-to-senior gains in cognitive development for students at the predominantly African American institution. This may suggest that the environments at certain colleges encourage higher levels of social interaction for majority students.

Compared with students who do not belong to Greek-letter social organizations, members of white fraternities score lower on end-of-the-first-year measures of reading comprehension, mathematics, critical thinking, and composite achievement (Pascarella, Edison, Whitt et al. In press). Sorority members showed similar, though less substantial, negative effects after the first year on these four measures with only the reading comprehension and composite achievement scores being statistically significant. For men of

TABLE 3

OUT-OF-CLASS ACTIVITIES ASSOCIATED WITH GAINS
IN KNOWLEDGE ACQUISITION AND APPLICATION

Activity	Impact
Amount of time spent studying	Positive
Amount of time spent socializing	Negative
Student-faculty interaction, especially when focused on substantive topics (e.g., research projects)	Positive
Time devoted to community service	Positive
Sorority membership	Mixed[a]
Fraternity membership	Negative
Peer interactions when focused on course content, discussing racial or ethnic issues	Positive
Holding a leadership position	Positive
Living in campus residence	Mixed[a]
Living in an academic theme residence	Positive
Tutoring other students	Positive

[a]The research is contradictory in this area; that is, some studies show that the activity is positively related to gains in knowledge acquisition and application, other studies indicate the activity is negatively related.

color fraternity membership exerted a modest positive influence on these outcomes (Pascarella, Edison, Whitt et al. In press).

According to Terenzini et al. (1995), "Both students' class related experiences *and* their out-of-class experiences made statistically significant and unique (if sometimes modest) contributions to the explanation of variations in intellectual orientations above and beyond students' pre-college traits and their experiences in other areas of college life" (p. 39) (see also Terenzini, Springer, Pascarella, and Nora In press). Students' out-of-class experiences uniquely explained 2 percent to 8 percent of the total variance. The combination of in-class and out-of-class experiences "also exert a modest *joint* effect, together explaining between 2 and 12 percent of the variance not attributable uniquely to any other college experience or to students' pre-college characteristics" (p. 40). Similarly, Terenzini, Springer, Pascarella, and Nora (1994) found that changes in students' first-year critical thinking abilities were "shaped uniquely and jointly" by multiple influences, both in and out of the classroom (p. 1). Similar findings were reported by Springer et al. (1995).

Volkwein, King, and Terenzini (1986) reported results

consistent with the above for transfer students to a large state university during their first year at the new institution on a dependent measure of intellectual skill development; however, the net association of out-of-class experiences was much smaller statistically than the amount of involvement in the classroom. Apparently, many dimensions of cognitive development have a social or interpersonal base (Pascarella and Terenzini 1991), suggesting that such gains may be a function of a "variety of student experiences, not just those that are part of the formal instructional program" (Terenzini et al. In press).

Knowledge acquisition and application

This section reviews the out-of-class factors that influence knowledge acquisition and application (table 3). One condition of knowledge acquisition is unequivocal: the more one studies, the more one learns (Pace 1979 1990). In fact, "every strictly 'cognitive' or 'academic' outcome except foreign-language ability is significantly associated with hours per week studying or doing homework" (Astin 1993b, p. 223).

Involvement in activities and time-on-task. Terenzini et al. (1995) found that the amount of time students spent socializing with friends was negatively related to interest in academic learning (i.e., willingness to work hard and enjoying challenges related to learning new concepts) during the first year of college. They also found that activities in which a student participates outside the classroom (e.g., involvement in art, theater, or music, or the number of nonassigned books that students read) contribute the most to their intrinsic value in learning (i.e., greater interest in learning for self-understanding than preparation for a career). However, use of the library had a negative effect on intrinsic interest in learning. Serow and Dreyden (1990) reported that grades and time devoted to community service were positively related to interest in learning. The studies of membership in fraternities and sororities are not conclusive with regard to achievement. On balance, it appears that sorority membership is positively related to achievement while membership in fraternities may be either neutral or negative (Center for the Study of the College Fraternity 1982 1992; Pike and Askew 1990).

Some studies have attempted to quantify knowledge acquisition using standardized measures. Out-of-class activities have been found to be negatively related to Verbal scores from the Graduate Record Examination (GRE), which can be considered a surrogate measure of knowledge acquisition. These activities include hours per week spent in volunteer work, class-related group projects, participating in intercollegiate athletics, hours per week spent attending classes, and being tutored. Tutoring other students, however, is positively correlated with GRE Quantitative performance, while time socializing with friends is positively correlated and receiving personal or psychological counseling is negatively correlated with GRE Analytical score (Pascarella and Terenzini 1991). Working (on campus, off campus, or not working at all) is not related to gains in reading comprehension or mathematics during the first year of college (Pascarella, Bohr et al. 1994).

Student-faculty contact. Student interaction with faculty members outside the classroom on a research project was positively related to the intrinsic value students find in learning (Terenzini et al. 1995). Kuh (1995) found that knowledge acquisition was more frequently associated with classroom, laboratory, and studio activities; for example, only a quarter of the senior respondents in the study linked knowledge acquisition with out-of-class experiences. Those experiences beyond the classroom associated with knowledge acquisition include student-faculty interaction (Wilson et al. 1975), such as seeking feedback about one's academic performance and collaboration on a research project (Kuh 1993a 1995; Springer et al. 1995; Wilson 1966).

Peer interactions. Among the peer interactions that foster learning are:

> *discussing course content with other students, working on group projects for classes, tutoring other students, participating in intramural sports, being a member of a social fraternity or sorority, discussing racial or ethnic issues, socializing with someone from a different racial or ethnic group, participating in a campus protest, being elected to a student office, and hours per week spent in socializing or in student clubs or organizations* (Astin 1993b, p. 385).

Peer teaching and participation in peer tutorial programs also have a positive impact on learning for those who do the teaching (Goldschmid and Goldschmid 1976). This is because students who teach other students must know the material more thoroughly than if they were only studying it for themselves (Annis 1983; Bargh and Schul 1980; Pace 1990). Moreover, such students become more actively engaged with the material to be taught which is thought to produce greater conceptual learning (Benware and Deci 1984; Pascarella and Terenzini 1991).

Pascarella et al. (1993) found that students who lived on campus exhibited greater (but nonstatistically significant) gains in reading and mathematics during the first year of college compared with those who commuted. Participation in intercollegiate athletics, especially men's sports of football and basketball, appears to be linked to smaller gains in reading comprehension and mathematical problem solving, compared with other students (Pascarella, Bohr, Nora, and Terenzini 1995).

Humanitarianism

This section summarizes the research related to the contributions of out-of-class activities to developing a deeper understanding and appreciation of human differences (table 4).

TABLE 4

OUT-OF-CLASS ACTIVITIES ASSOCIATED WITH GAINS IN HUMANITARIANISM

Activity	Impact
Discussing racial or ethnic issues	Positive
Socializing with people from different racial or ethnic groups	Positive
Attending racial or cultural awareness workshops (especially for white students)	Positive
Taking an interpersonal skills course	Positive
Study abroad	Positive
Participating in honors programs	Positive
Working part-time in a non-work-study, on-campus job	Positive
Experience as a paraprofessional	Positive
Social leadership activities	Positive
Formal and social interaction with faculty	Positive
Living in campus residences, especially coeducational settings	Positive
Fraternity membership for white male students	Negative

The need to understand and appreciate human differences has become more important as the characteristics of students participating in higher education has become more diverse. This cluster of outcomes includes cultivation of humanitarian attitudes, awareness of social and political views, increases in tolerance to a variety of viewpoints and people, and the broadening of interpersonal relations.

In general, out-of-class activities linked with increases in cultural awareness include discussing racial or ethnic issues (Astin 1993a 1993b; Kuh 1995), participating in a study-abroad program (Kauffmann and Kuh 1985), and holding a part-time, on-campus, non-work-study job (Astin 1993b). Astin (1993a 1993b) also found that cultural awareness and commitment to promoting racial understanding were most strongly influenced by such factors as attending racial or cultural awareness workshops and socializing with people from race or ethnic groups different from one's own. Similarly, Pascarella, Edison, Nora et al. (In press) found that openness to diversity after the first year of college was positively related to participation in a racial or cultural awareness workshop. This relationship was most pronounced for white students. However, membership in a fraternity or sorority had a negative effect on white students' openness to cultural diversity (Pascarella, Edison, Nora et al. In press).

Leadership activities. Social leadership activities (e.g., president of a student organization, committee work) are correlated with the development of humanitarian and civic values (Astin and Kent 1983; Kuh 1995; Kuh and Lund 1994; Pascarella, Ethington, and Smart 1988). Students who participated in a one-academic-credit-hour course that included relationship skills workshops taught by residence life staff improved their self-expression abilities and their active listening skills (Waldo 1989). In another study comparing groups of trained paraprofessionals who worked in a summer orientation program with an untrained pool of nonparticipants, Holland and Huba (1989) found statistically significant increases in the tolerance and interdependence of the paraprofessionals.

Student-faculty contact. Contact with faculty also has been associated with gains in humanitarianism. Using longitudinal CIRP data, Deppe (1989) concluded that mere proximity of people from different racial and ethnic groups had little influence on the development of constructive interpersonal relationships. Rather, formal and social involvement with faculty as well as academic program involvement played a critical role in the development of such social concern values as helping others in difficulty, participating in community action, and helping to promote racial understanding. For white students, involvement with faculty in out-of-class settings (e.g., going to a faculty member's home, out-of-class discussions) had the greatest impact. For African American students, academic program involvement (e.g., participation in an honors programs, opportunities to discuss course work and assignments out-of-class) had the greatest impact (Deppe 1989).

Living environments. Finally, living on campus is associated with liberalization of political views, support for civil liberties, enlightened racial attitudes, and broadening of interpersonal relationships (Pascarella and Terenzini 1991). Comparing single-sex and coeducational housing, Brown, Winkworth and Braskamp (1973) found that those living in coeducational settings more easily formed opposite-sex interpersonal relationships. Living in coeducational residences also has been linked to declines in sex-role stereotyping (Katz 1974). Molla and Westbrook (1990) found that white students who had positive residence hall roommate relationships with African American students expressed more positive attitudes towards African Americans in general compared with white students who had evaluated a similar experience as negative. Such outcomes, however, may be related more to the contacts between peers and faculty promoted by living on campus than to place of residence.

...living on campus is associated with liberalization of political views, support for civil liberties, enlightened racial attitudes, and broadening of interpersonal relationships.

Interpersonal and intrapersonal competence
This section summarizes the research on the links between out-of-class activities and the development of a coherent, integrated constellation of personal attributes such as self-esteem, confidence, values development, aesthetic appreciation, integrity, and civic responsibility [e.g., promoting the "common good" by voting and social or political activism (Knox, Lindsay, and Kolb 1993) (table 5)]. Self-esteem represents one's self-assessment of what one wishes to be contrasted with what one is in the present. Satisfaction with this

TABLE 5

OUT-OF-CLASS ACTIVITIES ASSOCIATED WITH GAINS IN INTERPERSONAL AND INTRAPERSONAL COMPETENCE

Activity	Impact
Involvement in voluntary service organizations	Postitive
Social leadership activities	Positive
Participation in intercollegiate athletics	Positive
Experience as a paraprofessional	Positive
Study abroad	Positive
Honors program participation	Positive
Out-of-class interaction with faculty	Positive
Living in campus residences, especially academic theme units and coeducational settings	Positive
Socializing with people from different racial or ethnic groups	Positive
Exposure to people with diverse perspectives	Positive
Exposure to and people with more advanced moral reasoning abilities	Positive
Fraternity or sorority membership	Mixed[a]

[a]The research is contradictory in this area; that is, some studies show that the activity is positively related to gains in interpersonal and intrapersonal competence, other studies indicate the activity is negatively related.

self-assessment leads to a generally positive or negative conceptualization of self. Confidence not only stems from a positive perception of self but also positive feedback about one's self from others. In addition, a student's feelings of social and academic competence can lead to a greater self-satisfaction and increased confidence. Taken together, these factors contribute to the formation of a person's identity and self-understanding.

Leadership activities. Participation in a variety of leadership activities has been linked with gains in students' intrapersonal competence. Evanoski (1988) found that community college students involved in a voluntary service organization (Student Orientation Leaders) reported increased feelings of self-satisfaction and confidence compared with those who did not participate. Participation in social leadership activities (e.g., president of a student organization, member of theatrical play cast, school publication board, or athletic team) has been linked to increases in self-concept, especially among women (Astin 1977; Astin and Kent 1983; Pascarella et al. 1987). Pascarella et al. (1987) also found the impact of participation in social leadership activities particularly important for self-concepts of African American, male students. According to Pascarella and Smart (1991), athletic participation had a statistically significant indirect and total effect on social self-esteem for African American students.

Kuh (1995) reported that seniors associated their gains in self-awareness, social competence, self-esteem, and autonomy with peer interactions, specific leadership responsibilities, and institutional ethos. Leadership experiences in particular (e.g., student government or fraternity officer, peer adviser) accounted for 45 percent of all gains in these areas. Similarly, experience in a paraprofessional role has been linked with gains in self-confidence, self-awareness, skills in interpersonal communication, and group dynamics. Finally, participation in an academic honors program (King 1973) and in a study abroad program (Kauffmann and Kuh 1985) also have been associated with increased self-esteem.

Student-faculty contact. Student-faculty interaction beyond the classroom is positively correlated with personal growth in the areas of leadership, social activism, and intellectual self-esteem (Astin 1993b), and academic self-concept as well as social self-concept (Astin and Kent 1983; Pascarella et al. 1987; Smart and Pascarella 1986). Such interactions include the hours per week spent talking with faculty outside of class, assisting faculty in teaching a class, working on a professor's research project, and being a guest in a professor's home. Faculty and students characterized effective teachers as those who made class interesting and were accessible to students outside of class (Wilson et al. 1975; Wilson, Wood, and Gaff 1974). Kuh (1995), however, found that only about 5 percent of the outcomes reported by students were attributed to contacts with faculty; women reported more such contacts and were more likely to attribute gains in interpersonal competence to these contacts.

Using the CIRP data base and a national survey of faculty, McHale (1994) found that faculty members with liberal attitudes tended to have a liberalizing effect on students' attitudes toward women; that is, the more students were exposed to faculty with liberal attitudes, the more egalitarian students became. Milem (1994) also reported a similar liberalizing influence of faculty-student interaction on student attitudes, using CIRP data.

Living environments. Finally, the nature and strength of certain residential experiences have been associated with gains in aspects of interpersonal and intrapersonal competence. Based on data from 14,600 students at 62 colleges from 1979 to 1982, Pace (1984) found that the largest differences in self-reported gains in personal and social development were between on-campus and off-campus students. Living-learning centers in particular appeared to have a positive influence on aesthetic appreciation (Blimling 1993); coeducational living environments are associated with declines in self-consciousness and anxiety in social settings (Reid 1974). Most of these gains are attributed to interactions with faculty and peers (Pascarella and Terenzini 1991). For example, students who live or spend time with someone from a different racial and ethnic background gain in appreciation for the aesthetic qualities of life (Astin 1993b). In addition, exposure to people with diverse perspectives and interaction with people who have more advanced stages of moral reasoning (e.g., discussions between first-year students and upper-class students or faculty members or staff, work-related experiences) have been shown to enhance moral reasoning abilities (Bertin, Ferrant, Whiteley, and Yokota 1985; Volker 1979; Whiteley 1980; Whiteley and Yokota 1988) and identity formation (Adams and Fitch 1983; Erwin and Delworth 1982; Henry and Renaud 1972; Komarovsky 1985; Madison 1969; Newman and Newman 1978).

Whiteley and Yokota's (1988) study of a living-learning center program (The Sierra Project) at the University of California, Irvine, found that intentionally integrating the curriculum with out-of-class experiences enhanced levels of principled thinking by first-year students. Exposure to people with diverse views is often developmentally challenging and contributes to the formation of personal identity—or the integration of such attributes as integrity, civic responsibility, aesthetic appreciation, confidence, and self-esteem. Involvement in activities. A secondary analysis of College Student Experiences Questionnaire (CSEQ) data collected by Kuh et al. (1991) found that gains in values development, self-understanding, teamwork, and developing health habits were related to involvement in social activities (Davis and Murrell 1993a). Whether identity and moral development are related to membership in fraternities and sororities is unclear (Kilgannon and Erwin 1992; Marlowe and Auvenshine 1982). Some evidence suggests that men who choose to join fraternities may have lower levels of moral reasoning at the start of college compared with those who do not join (Baier and Whipple 1990; Sanders 1990; Wilder, Hoyt, Surbeck, Wilder and Carney 1986).

Practical competence

This section summarizes research linking out-of-class experiences with the development of skills and competencies needed to be self-sufficient and successful in matters related to managing one's own affairs (e.g., time management, decision making), career development, and vocation (table 6). The influence of the out-of-class experience in the area of practical competence is broad, affecting areas as diverse as leadership development, occupational choice, decision-making skills, and feelings of personal competence (Evanoski 1988; Ethington, Smart, and Pascarella 1988; Kuh 1995; Kuh and Lund 1994).

TABLE 6

OUT-OF-CLASS ACTIVITIES ASSOCIATED WITH GAINS IN PRACTICAL COMPETENCE

Activity	Impact
Informal contact with faculty	Positive or none[a]
Involvement in voluntary service organizations	Positive
Social leadership activities	Positive
Participation in cocurricular activities	Positive or none[a]
Participation in intercollegiate athletics	Positive or none[a]
On- or off-campus employment, especially when directly related to academic major or vocational aspiration	Positive
Attendance at women's colleges	Positive or none[a]

[a]Studies indicate neither a positive nor negative relationship between the activity and gains in practical competence.

Student-faculty contact. Relationships between faculty and students have been shown to influence positively certain aspects of practical competence. Faculty-student informal contacts outside the classroom have a statistically significant influence on career choice, career interest, and eventual career selection (Astin 1977 1993b; Karman 1973; Komarovsky 1985; Wood and Wilson 1972). However, other aspects of practical competence (e.g., decision making, time management) do not seem to be influenced by contact with faculty (Kuh 1995).

Involvement in activities. Engagement in a wide variety of activities has been linked to career-development and vocational success. Students who volunteered to participate in a service organization reported gains in their sense of competence (Evanoski 1988), consistent with findings that practical competence is associated with leadership responsibilities (Kuh 1995; Kuh and Lund 1994). For example, leadership experiences (e.g., student government or fraternity officer, peer adviser) accounted for almost one quarter of all gains reported by seniors in this area (Kuh 1995).

The influence of involvement in cocurricular activities on occupational choice and attainment are equivocal. Weidman (1984) found that participating in co-curricular activities (e.g., student government, college organizations) did not have a direct effect on career choice. However, other studies (Braxton, Brier, Herzog, and Pascarella 1990; Ethington, Smart, and Pascarella 1988) suggest that extracurricular activities may have a significant effect on one's career. For example, Braxton et al. (1990) found that "experience in social leadership while attending college has a direct and positive [though small] influence on women becoming lawyers . . . , but not on men" (p. 294), a finding similar to that for women choosing science-related, sex-atypical careers (Ethington, Smart, and Pascarella 1988). Howard (1986) determined that cocurricular involvement did not predict occupational success for AT&T male managers. It was, however, related to assessments of managerial potential, especially participation in student government, involvement on a debating team, and serving on the school paper.

Involvement in intercollegiate athletics also shows mixed effects in relation to occupational status. Pascarella and Smart (1991) found that athletic participation was related to occupational status attainment for African American men and had a positive indirect effect on occupational status for Caucasian men, after controlling for race, socioeconomic background, occupational aspirations, college grades, and educational attainment. However, DuBois (1978) and Howard (1986), found trivial and statistically nonsignificant effects when comparing athletes and nonathletes.

Working during college, particularly in a job related to one's major or vocational goal, is related to subsequent career attainment (Pascarella and Terenzini 1991). For women, working during college solidifies their commitment to and interest in careers, as well as their choice of sex-atypical careers (Almquist and Angrist 1970 1971; Arnold 1987). Indeed, Kuh (1995) found that about one-third of the benefits seniors associated with their employment, either on or off campus, were in the practical competence domain (e.g., decision making, time management); work was especially important to students of color.

With regard to future earnings, some have reported that participation in cocurricular activities has a small, positive effect (Calhoon and Reddy 1968; Jepsen 1951; Walters and Bray 1963). However, Hunt (1963) found that involvement in cocurricular activities had a positive effect on earnings in one study, but a statistically nonsignificant effect for another group. Furthermore, participation in intercollegiate athletics was not related to postcollege earnings (DuBois 1978; Pascarella and Smart 1991).

Although studies of the influence of student involvement in co-curricular activities on career development are mixed, college graduates *think* such activities are important to their success after college; that is, college graduates typically refer to such involvement (e.g., leadership roles) as important to later achievements (Bisconti and Kessler 1980; Pascarella and Terenzini 1991; Schuh and Laverty 1983). However, it is likely that other variables (personality, motivation) may be more important in explaining such postcollege outcomes as income (Pascarella and Terenzini 1991).

Single-sex institutions. Finally, the influence of the gender composition of the institution on career outcomes is not clear. Tidball (1980 1986) and Tidball and Kistiakowsky (1976) discovered that graduates of women's colleges were more likely to enter male-dominated fields and had higher levels of occupational achievement than women from coeducational institutions. However, after controlling for students' background characteristics (something not done by Tidball), Stoecker and Pascarella (1991) determined that attendance at a women's college did not predict postcollege occupational attainment, concluding that "the career attainments previously linked to attendance at women's colleges may be attributable more to differential student recruitment than to socialization occurring in a distinctive institutional environment" (p. 403).

Summary

Out-of-class experiences affect students in myriad ways, many of which contribute directly or indirectly to persistence and to valued skills and competencies considered important outcomes of attending college. Kuh (1993a 1995); Terenzini, Springer, Pascarella, and Nora (1994); Volkwein, King, and Terenzini (1986); and others suggest that multiple and interrelated sources influence valued outcomes.

> *Academic and social effort expended by students are the principal determinants of the extent to which students themselves report that they grow and learn in college. Social effort is strongly influenced by academic effort, which suggests that for growth to occur, the work that is done in the classroom must find expression in other aspects of a student's life* (Davis and Murrell 1993a, p. 286).

The effects of college are cumulative and mutually shaping. For example, student cognitive growth seems to be influenced by a variety of experiences and conditions on a campus, particularly when out-of-class climates and experiences complement and encourage students to integrate what they learn in class with their lives outside the classroom (Kuh 1995). In addition, out-of-class activities that impact the development of cognitive skills also may impact the development of ethical and moral reasoning abilities. For example, ethical and moral reasoning abilities, sometimes referred to as principled thinking or reflective judgment (King and Kitchener 1994), are enhanced as cognitive skills increase (Cauble 1976; Faust and Arbuthnot 1978; Rowe and Marcia 1980). "This underscores the notion that moral development does not occur in isolation from other areas of student development during college but rather is a part of a network of mutually supporting changes" (Pascarella and Terenzini 1991, p. 366).

"Among the more powerful out-of-class experiences are those that demand sustained effort (e.g., planning, decision making) and require that students interact with people from different groups (e.g., faculty, administrators, trustees, employers) and peers from different backgrounds" (Kuh 1995, p. 145–46), particularly with regard to the development of practical competence skills. Life outside the classroom is an important venue that provides ample opportunities to synthesize and integrate material introduced in the formal academic program (classes, laboratories, studios), to test the value and worth of these ideas and skills, and to develop more sophisticated, thoughtful views on personal, academic, and other matters. This seems to be the case certainly for traditional-age students who live on campus:

> *[Students become] consumed, sometimes positively and sometimes negatively, with roommates and other relationships. The success of these relationships often affected the students' perceptions of themselves and the quality of their academic work. Involvement in organizations help students build confidence, learn skills, make career decisions, build friendships, develop leadership qualities, and feel comfortable. The tasks of everyday living and working yielded insights about individual functioning, responsibility to others, and values. Relationships with others in all of these contexts broadened students' perspectives about human diversity in their own place in the larger community* (Baxter Magolda 1992b, pp. 296–97).

Indeed, living in college housing contrasted with commuting to college is the "single most consistent within-college determinant of impact" (Pascarella and Terenzini 1991, p. 611), "shaping both the essential character and developmental impact of an individual's college experience" (Pascarella, Terenzini and Blimling 1994, p. 39). Those students who live on campus compared with their counterparts who commute: (a) participate in more extracurricular, social, and cultural events on campus; (b) interact more frequently with faculty and peers; (c) are more satisfied; (d) are more likely to graduate from college; and (e) exhibit greater gains in autonomy, intellectual orientation, self-concept, aesthetic, cultural, and intellectual values, and become more socially and politically open-minded (Pascarella, Terenzini, and Blimling 1994).

Contact beyond the classroom between faculty and students is key, fostering feelings of affirmation, confidence, and self-worth, particularly for women, and contributing to knowledge acquisition and the development of academic skills (Endo and Harpel 1982 1983; Pascarella 1980; Terenzini and Wright 1987; Volkwein, King, and Terenzini 1986; Wallace 1963 1967; Kuh 1995).

Whether gender or race and ethnicity is a factor in terms of what students learn outside the classroom is not clear. While some report systematic differences, others (MacKay and Kuh 1994; Pace 1990) say that these variables do not explain differences in undergraduate activities and outcomes. Apparently, what matters most in terms of benefiting from life outside the classroom is what one does. Whether students of color benefit more from contact with faculty and involvement in academic activities (MacKay and Kuh 1994) needs to be determined with greater precision.

With regard to most categories of benefits, student engagement is the key (Astin 1984; Friedlander 1980; Pace 1984; Parker and Schmidt 1982). That is, the benefits of out-of-class experiences depend not only upon what the institution does (or does not do) but also on the extent and quality of effort that the student puts into these activities (Pace 1980 1984 1990). This seems to be the case for students at commuter institutions as well (Abrahamowicz 1988).

Who students choose for friends and spend time with also is important (Kuh 1993c). "A large part of the impact of college is determined by the extent and content of one's interactions with major agents of socialization on campus, namely, faculty members and student peers" (Pascarella and Terenzini 1991, p. 620). According to Astin (1993b, p. 398), peers are "the single most potent source of influence," affecting virtually every aspect of development—cognitive, affective, psychological, and behavioral. Indeed, the differences in commuting to college and living in residences are more likely to be indirect influences (through the interactions that students have with agents of socialization) rather than direct; that is, transmitted by distinctive peer environments.

Student interaction with peers can positively influence overall academic development, knowledge acquisition, analytical and problem-solving skills, and self-esteem (Kuh 1993a 1995). Aleman (1994) found that "for female friends in college, conversations with each other serve as vehicles to transgress the limits of dualistic thinking" (p. 38). Female friendships may be models for peer-assisted learning, an "often neglected potent resource inherent in a student population" (Alexander, Gur, and Patterson 1974, p. 175).

CONDITIONS THAT FOSTER INVOLVEMENT IN EDUCATIONALLY PURPOSEFUL OUT-OF-CLASS ACTIVITIES

A good deal is known about the contributions of out-of-class experiences to student learning and personal development. Given this research, it is all the more surprising that the out-of-class environment is often ignored, overlooked, or discounted in terms of its impact on student learning. Colleges and universities can no longer afford to ignore the rich potential of out-of-class experiences in fostering student learning. Efforts are needed throughout the entire institution to transcend the artificial boundaries between classrooms, studios, and laboratories and other aspects of a student's life. The following section highlights nine conditions that, taken together, characterize a developmentally powerful out-of-class environment that fosters student learning and development.

Clear, Coherent, and Consistently Expressed Educational Purposes

Clear and consistent objectives, stated in terms of desired outcomes for learning and personal development, are critically important in creating an educationally powerful institution. These should not have to be deduced from course descriptions. They should be explicit and compelling. They should be defined by the members of the college community, taken to heart by campus leaders, and invoked as guides to decision-making (Chickering and Reisser 1993, p. 287).

An institution demonstrates its values in a variety of ways—what leaders say in public statements, where resources are allocated, and how faculty spend their time to name a few. Perhaps the most obvious place to look for what an institution is trying to accomplish is the mission statement. A clearly expressed mission statement is an important historical record, artifactual evidence of the institution's covenant with its supporters. But the enacted or living mission of an institution is not necessarily what it writes about itself. Moreover, "some institutions can be clear about their mission but not clear about what that mission implies for student learning and development" (Chickering and Reisser 1993, p. 284).

Like the rudder of a ship, the living mission of a college or university is what the institution does as it expresses its values and priorities concerning student learning through hundreds of thousands of daily interactions between administrators, faculty, staff, and students as well as celebratory events and public statements by institutional leaders. Many of the former are public acts; others are less visible but equally important in shaping the institution's character and what students discern as important and valuable ways of spending their time. When the living mission is coherent, consistently expressed, and congruent with the institution's espoused goals and aspirations, it becomes salient, shaping the views of outsiders toward the institution (Keeton 1971; Kuh et al. 1991). External constituents of a university with a salient, living mission are able to describe the institution in the same way students and faculty describe the institution. Moreover, a living mission is a compass of sorts, sending signals to students, faculty, and others about how to behave, articulating what a college or university is and aspires to be, and keeping the institution on track through troubled times.

The living mission is particularly useful with regard to out-of-class experiences when it explicitly addresses the importance of certain types of activities over others. For example, how is the living mission of a college manifested in residence halls, student government, and student organizations? How is the living mission used to guide assessments of out-of-class learning and personal development? Is the institutional mission used to lead out-of-class improvement efforts? Discussion on these questions, and many more like them, form the bases upon which an educationally powerful environment for student learning takes hold.

An Institutional Philosophy that Embraces a Holistic View of Talent Development

A variety of mutually shaping experiences inside and outside the classroom influence student learning. Just as the living mission gives direction to people concerning an institution's educational goals, its philosophy represents the preferred approach to performing the tasks necessary to attain the goals. That is:

> *An institution's philosophy is the means (policies, practices, standard operating procedures) by which its mission is enacted. Although many colleges do not explicitly articulate their philosophy (e.g., describe "how things are done here" in the catalogue or mission statement), the assump-*

tions and beliefs about human potential, teaching, and learning on which the college's philosophy is based can be discovered through examining such documents as catalogs and mission statements, talking with members of various constituent groups (e.g., students, faculty, graduates, trustees), and observing how routine business is transacted (Kuh 1991a, p. 12).

Learning outside the classroom is most likely to flourish when an institution adopts a holistic view of student learning and development and adopts talent development as an institutional goal. "The most excellent institutions are . . . those that have the greatest impact—'add the most value,' as economists would say—on the student's knowledge and personal development and on the faculty member's scholarly and pedagogical ability and productivity" (Astin 1985, p. 61).

Institutions that embrace a talent development philosophy also recognize and respect the diverse talents that students from various backgrounds and cultures bring to the learning environment (Chickering and Gamson 1987). Each student adds to the learning process a unique knowledge base and view of the world. Through sharing their knowledge and experience, students enrich the learning of others as well as their own (Alexander and Murphy 1994). "Faculty who show regard for their students' unique interests and talents are likely to facilitate student growth and development in every sphere—academic, social, personal, and vocational" (Sorcinelli 1991, p. 21).

For many institutions, adopting a holistic talent development philosophy will require a shift in focus from teaching courses and offering degree programs to viewing student learning as a combination of intellectual and social experiences that occur both inside and outside the classroom (Astin 1985; Kuh et al. 1991; Vincow 1993). Faculty and staff must make it a priority to help students reflect on and seek connections among these experiences.

Learning outside the classroom is most likely to flourish when an institution adopts a holistic view of student learning and development...

Complementary Institutional Policies and Practices Congruent with Students' Characteristics and Needs

Institutions enact their mission and philosophy through formal and informal policies and practices that encourage or discourage student participation in educationally purposeful activities beyond the classroom.

Virtually every institutional policy and practice . . . can
affect the way students spend their time and the amount
of effort they devote to academic pursuits. Moreover,
administrative decisions about many nonacademic issues
. . . can significantly affect how students spend their time
and energy (Astin 1984, p. 302).

Students make judgments about real world problems as
they watch and listen to others in classes, on playing fields,
over meals, and in the residence hall (King and Kitchener
1994). As a result, teachable moments are in ample supply
outside the classroom, ranging from disagreements between
roommates to heated debates and protests related to sexual
orientation, free speech, and political issues. Although some
stakeholders (e.g., governing board members, presidents,
many parents) prefer a tranquil institution, potent learning
environments are rarely without occasional controversy. In
order to foster intellectual development through such
exchanges, however, different points of view must be examined in a reflective manner (King and Kitchener 1994). An
institution that values out-of-class learning does not consider
such events to be distractions but as opportunities for faculty
and students to practice effective citizenship skills and apply
what they are learning in their classes to their lives outside
the classroom.

Often the talents of students from diverse backgrounds
(e.g., ethnic and racial minorities, adult learners, students
with learning disabilities) are misunderstood, ignored, or
devalued. Too many faculty and staff interpret cultural and
learning style differences to be academic deficiencies in
need of remediation (Pounds 1987). Treisman (1992) noted
that many students from historically underrepresented
groups at University of California–Berkeley were failing calculus even though they had the academic prerequisites and
demonstrated ability to perform successfully. He discovered
that environmental disorientation was the problem, not lack
of motivation as was assumed initially by their instructors.
Treisman (1992) developed strategies so that these African
American and Hispanic students could use and further hone
their mathematical and problem-solving talents. "We did not
question that minority students could excel. We just wanted
to know what kind of setting we would need to provide so

that they could" (Treisman 1992, p. 368). By adopting a talent-development perspective and taking into account the backgrounds and characteristics of the students, Treisman and his colleagues were able to develop a model program that is responsive to the needs of a variety of students.

High, Clear Expectations for Student Performance

During the past decade various national reports have emphasized the importance of expectations on student performance (Chickering and Gamson 1987; National Association of Student Personnel Administrators 1995; Study Group 1984). For example, the Wingspread Group (1993) suggested that faculty, academic administrators, and student affairs staff raise educational expectations as a means of improving student learning. Similarly, Linda Wilson (1992), the president of Radcliffe College, observed that the single greatest challenge facing American higher education is to raise its aspirations and those of its students.

High, clearly communicated expectations for students are important for at least three reasons. First, they specify the desired level of performance for students, faculty, and staff. A shift occurred in the late 1960s in the nature of relations between students and their institution when the in loco parentis doctrine was set aside by legal challenges. "Most institutions, however, did not develop a coherent set of expectations to replace in loco parentis, relying instead on civil law to define the institution-student relationship" (National Association of Student Personnel Administrators 1995, p. 1).

Second, statements of institutional expectations in areas such as student achievement, extent and intensity of involvement in various activities, and standards for academic and personal behavior signal to students that the institution wants them to succeed. "Expect more and you will get more. High expectations are important for everyone—for the poorly prepared, for those unwilling to exert themselves, and for the bright and well motivated" (Chickering and Gamson 1987, pp. 67-68). In this sense, expectations for achievement become a self-fulfilling prophecy (Jussim 1986), motivating students to perform in the desired ways and conveying a message of success. Some caution is needed, however, to express expectations for student performance in such a way so as to not create conditions that are overly stressful, intimidating, or constraining for students (Kuh et al. 1991).

Third, faculty affirm students' goals and abilities by holding them to high standards of performance. As a result, students are more likely to see merit and worth in staying in college and, thus, benefit to a greater degree from the college experience (Kuh et al. 1991; Pascarella and Terenzini 1991).

Although these arguments are compelling, little empirical evidence exists to demonstrate the link between high expectations and student performance in postsecondary settings (National Center for Higher Education Management Systems 1993). The absence of data contrasts sharply with the wealth of empirical studies on this topic at the K-12 level (Brophy and Good 1974; Jussim 1986). The evidence regarding the positive effect of high teacher expectations on student satisfaction is unequivocal, however. High expectations lead to greater student satisfaction with their courses and higher ratings of their instructors (Sorcinelli 1991), a conclusion drawn by others as well (e.g., Cashin 1988; Marsh 1984). After examining teaching and learning at Harvard University, Light (1990, 1992) concluded that students appreciated most those classes characterized by high faculty demands and standards, particularly when students were able to revise and improve their work before grading.

Thus, there is sufficient reason to believe—based on studies at the K-12 level and our knowledge of good teaching and learning practices—to conclude that although high expectations cannot assure student success, low expectations are almost always deleterious (Kuh 1993c; National Association of Student Personnel Administrators 1995).

Use of Effective Teaching Approaches
Bruffee (1995) describes education as an acculturation process, where individuals learn how to "share their toys" with other students, and in turn other individuals throughout their lifetime.

> *The main purpose of primary school education is to help children renegotiate their membership in the local culture of family life and help them join some of the established knowledge communities available to them and the encompassing culture we hold in common. An important pur-*

pose of college or university education is to help adoles-
cents and adults join some more of the established knowl-
edge communities available to them. But another, and
perhaps more important purpose of college or university
education is to help students renegotiate their membership
in the encompassing common culture that until then has
circumscribed their lives (Bruffee 1995, p. 15).

Therefore, the most important thing that any faculty member can do is to create those environments in which students learn the course content through their interactions with others. Another term for this concept is collaborative learning.

Collaborative learning is an approach to teaching effectively that has become more popular in the 1980s and the 1990s. "Collaborative learning is an umbrella term for a variety of educational approaches involving joint intellectual effort by students, or students and teachers together. In most collaborative learning situations students are working in groups of two or more, mutually searching for understanding, solutions, or meanings, or creating a product" (Smith and MacGregor 1992, p. 10). There are many different collaborative learning approaches including cooperative learning, problem-centered instruction, writing groups, peer teaching, discussion groups and seminars, and learning communities (Christensen 1987; McKeachie, Pintrich, Lin, and Smith 1986; Kulik, Kulik, and Cohen 1980; Palmer 1987; Shor 1992; Smith and MacGregor 1992).

Of the five approaches, cooperative learning is the most structured type of collaborative learning. Collaborative learning is based on a set of five assumptions about learning:

1. Learning is an active, constructive process.
2. Learning depends on rich contexts.
3. Learners are diverse.
4. Learning is inherently social.
5. Learning has affective and subjective dimensions (Smith and MacGregor 1992, p. 10-11).

These assumptions about learning are based on student outcomes research which shows that students gain more when they are actively involved in the learning process. For example, Astin's (1993b) work shows that two environmental factors significantly predict positive change in student

learning outcomes: (1) interaction among students, and (2) interaction between faculty and students (Smith, Johnson, and Johnson 1992). Cooperative learning approaches require that teachers monitor the students more closely with the goal of having students learn how to work well with others socially. Rather than holding students accountable individually, collaborative learning demands student involvement, cooperation and teamwork, and civic responsibility (Smith and MacGregor 1992). Thus, "collaborative learning replaces the traditional classroom social structure with another structure: negotiated relationships among students and a negotiated relationship between those student communities and the teacher" (Bruffee 1995, p. 17).

As a result, we could say, collaborative learning in colleges and universities complements the cooperative learning that children may experience in primary school. With regard to the educational career of any individual person, collaborative learning is designed to pick up where cooperative learning leaves off. The principle remains substantially the same. The emphasis changes (Bruffee 1995, p. 16).

In addition to collaborative learning, a good deal is known about teaching approaches that are effective in fostering higher levels of learning. For example:

1. Good teachers are knowledgeable about their subject matter, are enthusiastic, encourage students to express their views through discussion, and interact with their students, both in and outside of class (Feldman 1976; Marsh 1984; McKeachie et al. 1986; Murray 1985; Pascarella 1980);
2. Students learn more from courses when they are given timely feedback that is both supportive and corrective (Cross 1987; McKeachie et al. 1986; Menges and Mathis 1988; Kulik, Kulik, and Cohen 1980);
3. When students are expected to work hard, academic achievement, class attendance, and their sense of responsibility all increase (Berliner 1984; Cashin 1988; Marsh 1984); and
4. Because every student learns differently, individualized instruction is more effective under most circumstances (McKeachie et al. 1986).

It seems reasonable to assume that if these effective approaches were adapted by faculty, administrators, student affairs staff, and others who routinely interact with students outside the classroom (e.g., faculty advisers to organizations, internship supervisors, employers, peer mentors) out-of-class experiences would make a greater contribution to students' learning and personal development and increase institutional productivity.

Systematic Assessment of Institutional Practices and Student Performance

Institutions that take seriously student learning outside the classroom regularly assess the relationships between student involvement in various out-of-class activities and events, outcomes, and institutional policies and practices. One example is monitoring what students do with their time when they are not in class (e.g., how much time they spend studying compared with other activities). The American Association of Higher Education's Assessment Forum (1992) recommends that assessments be based on the following principles:

1. Be certain that assessment approaches (data collection, interpretation) are congruent with the institution's educational values;
2. Use data collection and analysis approaches that are multidimensional and integrated;
3. Clearly state the purposes and intended uses of the assessment;
4. Emphasize in the data collection and interpretation both outcomes and processes that are associated with the outcomes;
5. Conduct assessments on an ongoing, not an episodic, basis;
6. Involve people from different parts of the institution in various aspects of the assessment;
7. Focus on issues considered important by the people to be affected by the results;
8. Coordinate and integrate assessment activities with other institutional improvement efforts; and
9. Use assessment information to demonstrate accountability to various constituencies.

The fourth principle is particularly important if out-of-class learning experiences are to be integrated with curricular goals. Process indicators can help determine whether the conditions are present (e.g., student time-on-task, student-faculty interactions, high expectations) that lead to desired outcomes (Banta 1993; Ewell and Jones 1993; National Center for Higher Education Management Systems 1993). Knowledge of the processes associated with various outcomes helps educators identify the types of activities and experiences that enhance learning so they can use their time more productively by addressing these processes. Locally developed or standardized tests can be expensive and difficult to administer (Banta 1993). In contrast, process indicators have the advantages of being less difficult and expensive to develop and implement; also, they are action-oriented in that they can be used immediately to inform policy decisions that would enhance student learning (Ewell and Jones 1993). Finally, process indicators reflect the complex relations among in-class and out-of-class interactions that lead to student learning and development.

Ample Opportunities for Student Involvement in Educationally Purposeful Out-of-Class Activities

"Learning is strongly influenced by the degree to which an individual is invested in the learning process" (Alexander and Murphy 1994, p. 12). Thus, the amount of time and effort students devote to various activities warrant attention.

Providing diverse events and activities that appeal to students is necessary but not sufficient. That is, the mere availability of such opportunities does not ensure that students will take advantage of them. To increase student involvement in educationally purposeful out-of-class activities, colleges and universities must assist students in maximizing the learning potential of such opportunities and seek ways in which to intentionally engage students. This is especially important for those (e.g., women, students of color) who perceive that certain opportunities are not open to people like them. "Institutions must work to create a climate in which all students feel welcome and able to fully participate" (Davis and Murrell 1993, p. iii).

Students, staff, and faculty often limit their thinking about educationally purposeful out-of-class opportunities to institutionally recognized activities and groups or formalized student leadership positions. One result is that student affairs professionals and others typically devote a disproportionate share of time to groups and organizations that the institution has traditionally acknowledged as important to campus life, such as student government and fraternities. There are many reasons why such groups warrant attention (e.g., they provide opportunities for students to exercise responsibility and sponsor social activities). However, anecdotal evidence indicates that fewer students seem to be participating in this "formal extracurriculum" (Moffatt 1989). A broader view of involvement and leadership is needed, one that encourages students to exercise responsibility but not constrained to traditional roles such as formally recognized groups, e.g., student government or fraternities and sororities (Anchors, Douglas, and Kasper 1993). Informal leaders can be equally influential on their peers, the campus climate, and intended learning outcomes. For example, a student who decides to write a letter to the school newspaper to voice a concern can initiate change on campus. Also, many commuter students organize informal social activities, study groups, car pools, and child care arrangements. Thus, more attention must be given to the informal student groups that form and the activities in which members of these groups are involved.

Balancing engagement in a variety of both in- and out-of-class experiences is critical to maximizing positive outcomes (Kuh 1981). Although "the level of students' involvement in the institutional environment is positively related to value change, it has also been shown that too much involvement may be counterproductive" (Pascarella and Terenzini 1991, p. 313). Students who limit their involvement solely to academics do not show the same gains as students who are involved in a broader range of activities (Astin 1984). Athletes who limited their involvement to primarily experiences associated with their sport also failed to show similar gains. Limiting involvement to any one portion of the collegiate experience appears to reduce the amount and type of change that a student can realize.

Prompt feedback also is important for fostering environments focused on achievement and growth on a variety of valued dimensions (Chickering and Gamson 1987). Recall that prompt feedback in the classroom is related to gains in student achievement and satisfaction (McKeachie et al. 1986), especially when the feedback is corrective, supportive, and immediate (Sorcinelli 1991). These same conditions should hold for out-of-class settings.

Human Scale Settings Characterized by Ethics of Membership and Care

Creating and maintaining human scale settings are critical to engaging students in educationally purposeful activities. As Chickering and Reisser (1993) pointed out, "Small size, both in absolute number and the ratio of persons to opportunities and pressure for active participation, is important" (p. 406). However, small size itself does not cause student involvement, though it almost certainly increases the likelihood of engagement (Kuh 1981). Small group size typically encourages greater interpersonal involvement. Indeed, "a large part of the impact of college is determined by the extent and content of one's interactions with major agents of socialization on campus, namely, faculty members and student peers" (Pascarella and Terenzini 1991, p. 620).

Institutions marked by human scale settings seem to encourage student engagement in a variety of activities. From their study of *Involving Colleges,* Kuh et al. (1991) distilled five factors that foster engagement in educationally purposeful activities: (a) a welcoming physical environment, (b) a psychological environment that seeks to balance challenge and support, (c) the presence of safe spaces that allow for personal reflection, (d) the absence of anonymity, and (e) support for multiple subcommunities to form and flourish. Human scale settings feel comfortable and manageable (i.e., small colleges seem larger and large universities seem smaller). Indoor and outdoor spaces (e.g., classrooms, student lounges, pedestrian malls) are arranged to foster informal, spontaneous interaction among students and students and faculty. "Moreover [at Involving Colleges], such opportunities for meaningful involvement as leadership positions in student organizations and campus governance structures are in ample supply" (Kuh 1991a, p. 16).

The most critical issue regarding campus environments and student involvement is . . . creating a sense of belonging, a feeling on the part of the students that the institution acknowledges the human needs of social and psychological comfort, and that they are full and valued members of the campus community (Kuh et al. 1991, p. 321).

Ideally, colleges and universities are caring communities. "To care and be cared for are fundamental human needs" (Noddings 1992, p. xi). "As impossible as the goal may seem to be, a modern college or university should be a place where every individual feels affirmed and where every activity of the community is humane. Caring is the key" (Carnegie Foundation for the Advancement of Teaching 1990, p. 47). At institutions marked by ethics of care and membership people sense that they belong, that they "matter to someone else, that they are the object of someone else's attention, and that others care about them and appreciate them" (Schlossberg, Lynch, and Chickering 1989, p. 2).

Among other things, this "ethic of care" means that students are appreciated for what they bring to the institution; they are not seen as a drain on institutional resources or an unwelcome diversion of faculty attention from research and scholarly activity. . . . newcomers . . . behave as full members of the community with all attendant rights and responsibilities. Moreover, this "ethic of membership" sends a clear message to students . . . "you are here because we believe you can succeed" (Kuh 1991a, p. 13).

For students to be successful and feel valued, they must have their interests and heritage acknowledged, legitimated, and appreciated. At the same time, for student growth and learning to occur students must be challenged as well as supported, academically and socially (Sanford 1962). Subcommunities, or small groups of people with similar interests, typically form naturally on larger campuses. Creating a campus climate where distinctive subcommunities can coexist harmoniously is especially important on small campuses where the culture compels people to conform. Distinctive subcommunities can not only provide for but also possibly encourage productive debate and dialogue.

An Ethos of Learning that Pervades All Aspects of the Institution

"Ethos (from the Greek, "habit") is a belief system widely shared by faculty, students, administrators, and others. It is shaped by a core of educational values manifested in the

For students to be successful and feel valued, they must have their interests and heritage acknowledged, legitimated, and appreciated.

institution's mission and philosophy" (Kuh 1993b, p. 22). Yet the role of an institution's ethos in shaping behavior receives little attention in the higher education literature (Kuh 1993b) even though ethos and other cultural properties influence learning and personal development (Davis and Murrell 1993a; Kuh et al. 1991; Pratt and McLaughlin 1989). In part ethos receives little attention because it is difficult to define clearly. In this sense, the words of jazz immortal Louis Armstrong are relevant. When asked to define jazz, Armstrong replied that "I know it when I hear it. . . . And if I have to explain it to you, you'll never get it."

An institution's ethos and related cultural properties warrant attention because students at institutions characterized by an ethos of learning show greater gains in learning and personal development than students at other institutions (Kuh et al. 1991; Kuh, Vesper, and Krehbiel 1994). At these institutions, the institutional culture communicates to students, faculty, and staff—at a deep, almost unconscious level—the central role of learning at the college or university. These institutions are characterized by an environment in which "learners are known by name and respected as individuals, feel comfortable, interact with people from backgrounds different from their own, feel free to take intellectual risks, assume responsibility for their learning and social welfare, and have opportunities to participate in community governance" (National Association of Student Personnel Administrators 1995, p. 8). Such an ethos develops as a result of an intentional focus on student achievement by faculty and staff. They reflect on and frequently discuss among themselves and with their students the central role of learning in their lives and for the institution.

Colleges and universities that reflect to varying degrees the preceding eight conditions are well on their way to engendering an ethos of learning. They are similar in some important ways to "learning organizations." They value learning because it is an inexhaustible source of renewal and innovation. They encourage all of their members to "continually expand their capacity to create the results they truly desire, where new and expansive patterns of thinking are nurtured, where collective aspiration is set free, and where people are continually learning how to learn together" (Senge 1990, p. 3). Hill (1994), borrowing a phrase from Walter Lippmann (1984), described this situation as "the hospitality of the inquiring mind . . . one that invites ideas in, asks them to sit down, talks with them for a while, and makes them feel at home. They may leave, but there has been an engagement" (Hill 1994, p. 9). This personification of the inquiring mind is, at the same time, the type of engagement that faculty members, student affairs staff, and other educators must encourage and expect from students.

A college or university with an ethos of learning draws in students, compelling them to examine affirming and challenging ideas and perspectives and encouraging them to reflect, ponder, question, debate, and act on their learning. Such institutions value debate, discussion, and the free flow of ideas without regard to topic. They promote programs and avenues through which students may reflect on and make connections between life activities and their larger educational experience, both on and off campus (Kuh, Vesper, and Krehbiel 1994). Indeed, many students at certain types of institutions (metropolitan universities, community colleges) spend relatively little time at their institution. These students often work elsewhere, are engaged in community service, and devote much of their discretionary time to their families, churches, and neighborhood organizations. Said another way, an ethos of learning is not place bound, but is a deeply held belief in holistic talent development unaffected by the institution's physical or psychological boundaries, reputational rank, or size of endowment.

IMPLICATIONS

This section offers suggestions for those committed to creating learning opportunities for undergraduate students outside the classroom. Any institution can improve student learning by using its existing resources more effectively to create the conditions under which students learn best, both inside and outside the classroom. Knowledge, will, and commitment are the key factors, not money.

At most colleges and universities the current organizational arrangements of academic and student affairs, academic departments, business affairs, and other units have become "functional silos" (Marchese 1994), inhibiting collaboration and cooperation that could advantage students in using the institution's resources for learning. Breaking down these barriers is a key challenge. Thus, student learning outside the classroom must be everyone's business. That is, only through collaboration among administrators, faculty, student affairs staff, and students can a college or university create an ethos of learning that supports and encourages participation in the kinds of activities that must be pursued with vigor and enthusiasm to create the other necessary conditions.

Experience shows that when responsibility belongs to everyone, few take the responsibility seriously enough to devote the energy and time needed to change the status quo. However, if some persons or groups are held accountable for implementing specific policies and practices, changes in behavior, beliefs, and attitudes are more likely to occur. For student learning outside the classroom to be more tightly connected to the institution's educational purposes, everyone must do their share but leadership, authority, and accountability must be exercised by designated institutional agents. That group should include the president as well as others in a position to shape the institution's culture and revise key policies and practices including the reward system (e.g., academic deans, student affairs administrators, faculty and student leaders).

To create the conditions described in the preceding section, we begin with some general recommendations. Then, some specific implications are discussed according to familiar primary role functions in a college or university— governing board member, president, academic administrator, faculty member, student affairs professional, and student.

General Recommendations

1. Cultivate an ethos of learning throughout the institution

Institutions with an ethos of learning are blessed with more than a few boundary spanners, people who move among the functional silos, articulating the institution's mission and vision with language that acknowledges and respects both classroom and out-of-class learning. To establish an ethos of learning, a multiple-year action plan is needed that brings together faculty members, student affairs staff, and academic administrators in collaborative, mutually supportive efforts. The goal is to extend the influence of academic programs beyond the boundaries of the classrooms, laboratories, studios, and faculty offices into the residences, student organizations, and institutional facilities.

Key to the success of the plan is fashioning institutional policies and practices that actively engage students in their learning by motivating them to use the educational resources already available. How can faculty, academic administrators, and student affairs staff work together to harness the energy and influence of peers to encourage students to put forth more effort that will result in the kinds of learning gains that are compatible with the institution's mission and students' educational and vocational objectives? Another goal is to create the conditions where all people feel welcome and comfortable so that they can take advantage of the institution's resources for learning. One such resource is human diversity.

Recent research (Astin 1993a 1993b) suggests that for students to reap the many educational benefits of a diverse campus community an institution's commitment must be fourfold: (a) to advance knowledge and intellectual understanding of differences among all groups (e.g., students, faculty, staff); (b) to encourage interaction among members of different groups (e.g., ethnic, cultural, gender-based, sexual orientation, academic interest); (c) to promote the appreciation and valuing of commonalities across all students; and (d) to build on commonalities while acknowledging and respecting the unique contributions that members of different groups make to an academic community.

There are sound educational reasons for such efforts. For example, students who live or spend time with someone from a different racial and ethnic background gain in understanding of human differences and appreciation for the aesthetic qualities of life (Astin 1993a 1993b). Toward these ends, public discussions are needed to determine how an institution can develop an environment marked by the ethics of care and membership described earlier so that all students feel welcome and succeed academically and socially.

As with other powerful learning experiences, there is no substitute for personal contact for encouraging student involvement in educationally purposeful activities. That is, the mere presence of involvement opportunities that appeal to a diversity of student needs and interests is not enough to ensure that students will take advantage of these opportunities. Faculty, student affairs staff, academic administrators and others encourage student effort through what may to some seem like insignificant gestures—comments in the margin of a student's essay acknowledging a salient point, words of encouragement after class or organizational meeting, a query about a student's well-being and educational progress, notes to students who have attained significant achievements, and many, many other expressions of interest and concern consistent with the institution's educational purposes and values. The confluence of these expressions of interest help students feel valued and encourages them to perform at a high level, both in and out of the classroom (Kuh et al. 1991).

2. Address the importance of out-of-class experiences explicitly in the institution's mission

The value of out-of-class experiences to attaining the institution's educational purposes warrants debate and discussion. No single best answer exists. Only through dialogue on this topic can faculty, staff, and students develop a shared vision of the enterprise—what the purposes of the institution are, what the students want from their college experience and the activities in which they should engage to attain their goals, what behaviors are expected of students, and what qualities characterize a healthy, effective academic community. Just as values decay over time (Gardner 1990), so it is with the collective understanding of institutional mission and purpose. Therefore, a concise statement is needed that describes what the student experience outside the classroom should be. Periodic discussions are needed to affirm and, if necessary, modify the understanding of what people are trying to accomplish together and to maintain clarity of purpose and a common view of how out-of-class experiences contribute to attaining the institution's purposes.

One approach to examining the mission with respect to the importance of learning outside the classroom is to pose the following question: What is this institution for? At first blush the query seems sophomoric. Yet it is precisely the differing answers various groups offer that create the contradictions, confusion, and misunderstandings about the role of out-of-class experiences in attaining the institution's educational purposes. The appropriate role of life outside the classroom will vary from institution to institution, depending in part on student characteristics and the institutional mission. The key is sharing knowledge about the potential contributions of out-of-class experiences to the desired outcomes of college and how the institution's educational resources can be used toward these ends. This means that many people must be intimately acquainted with the research literature summarized earlier.

3. Establish a holistic approach to talent development as the institution's philosophy of undergraduate education

A holistic talent development philosophy of education is essential to establish an ethos of learning that encourages students to take advantage of out-of-class learning opportunities. Institutions that adopt this view minimize role distinctions by encouraging everyone to consider themselves educators. At larger colleges and universities the talent development perspective will need to be interpreted at various organizational levels (i.e., academic departments, residence halls) to ensure that this philosophy guides thought and practice throughout the institution.

The magnitude of this task should not be underestimated. For example, many colleges and universities have become reluctant to engage in the lives of students following the demise of the in loco parentis doctrine that shaped student-institution relations. The absence of a guiding institutional compact has had deleterious effects in academic policies and practices as well. Increasing class sizes and the widespread use of the lecture as the dominant instructional approach favors anonymity, suggesting to students that they need not be actively engaged in the learning process. Many faculty members are reluctant to require class attendance. Symbolically, this practice suggests to students that class attendance is unimportant and they can shirk responsibility. Students who do not attend class do not benefit as much; also, many students have more discretionary time, which they do not always use to educational advantage.

4. Periodically assess the impact of the out-of-class environment on students

Few enterprises know less about their clients than institutions of higher education. In many institutions, the aspirations, backgrounds, abilities, and role orientation(s) (student, parent, worker) of students are very different from undergraduates of a decade or two ago. The institutional research office or student affairs division should collect and disseminate information about student characteristics, including data on specific student populations (e.g., members of historically underrepresented groups). At the same time, one needs to exercise caution in generalizing from composite information about student characteristics and experiences to individual students. Every student is unique, with unique needs, interests, and priorities. Members of certain subcommunities of students have needs specific to their group as well (Kuh et al. 1991).

In addition to cognitive development and knowledge acquisition, assessment efforts must address difficult-to-measure areas such as maturity, self-understanding, practical competence, tolerance, and humanitarianism. "These characteristics—which go beyond the intellectual impact—are perhaps among the most important college outcomes, and yet it is difficult, certainly in the short run, to determine whether these goals have been accomplished" (Boyer 1987, p. 260). As Astin (1991) observed, little progress will be made until institutions suspend efforts that value only that which can be measured, and focus instead on measuring what they value.

Another way to assess the impact of the out-of-class experience is to examine process indicators, such as "the extent to which the undergraduate has engaged in extracurricular activities and fulfilled . . . service requirements" (Boyer 1987, p. 261). Students might compile a portfolio or transcript reflecting their cocurricular, student leadership, and cultural experiences (Brown and DeCoster 1982).

Cocurricular transcripts are one way of emphasizing to students the importance of participation in certain out-of-class activities. In the past, cocurricular transcripts often did not include outcomes data, but simply listed the activities in which students participated during college. Thus, it is imperative that the benefits associated with participation in these activities be estimated and recorded.

Toward this end, existing structures (e.g., residence halls) and processes (e.g., new student orientation, academic advising) must be examined to determine whether they intentionally promote involvement in educationally purposeful activities. Too many structures and processes have become administrative, rather than educational, in character and function. For example, orientation and academic advising are often merely processing students and course matching respectively. Because of the significant human and fiscal resources directed to these activities, they must be re-engineered to focus on student learning. In this sense, orientation must be thought of as the primary social and academic integrating experience for newcomers and advising must emphasize educational planning and the skills needed to produce an academic plan that will realize the student's educational and personal goals as well as the institution's expectations.

Data on the impact of out-of-class experiences on student learning and development are needed to improve these and other programs and services, as well as to demonstrate the importance of out-of-class environments in enhancing student learning. These data can also be used to help shift the focus—especially for student affairs staff—from what services and programs are provided to what students are learning and how they are developing. In addition, this information can be used to document the contributions of the out-of-class environment to the many goals and values of an institution. Finally, information about how students use their time beyond the classroom can be a barometer of the extent to which faculty and staff use best practices in undergraduate education (Chickering and Gamson 1987). For example, clusters of items from the College Student Experiences Questionnaire (Pace 1990) reveal the amount of time and energy students devote to interactions with faculty, peers, and active learning, activities known to be directly linked to student learning (Kuh, Vesper and Pace 1995; Pace 1995).

5. Develop a common view of "what matters" in undergraduate education

Many definitions exist of what constitutes learning (Fincher 1985) In part this explains why faculty continually debate the most important outcomes of undergraduate education. Such debates are healthy if they lead to examinations of time-honored approaches to undergraduate education that are less productive (e.g., lecture) than other approaches (e.g., active learning) and of the mental models that reinforce these less productive behaviors. Mental models are "tacit assumptions (unquestioned beliefs behind all decisions and actions) and hidden cultures (shared but unwritten rules for each member's behavior)" (Kilmann 1984, p. 8) that shape the way people perceive the world and affect how they behave (Senge 1990). Most people are unaware of their mental models and how they influence their behavior.

Faculty, staff, and students have different mental models (Senge 1990) of what is important in undergraduate learning and personal development. That is, what a faculty member values most may differ greatly from those of staff members and students. Discovering these models and the assumptions and values they represent is necessary if faculty, academic administrators, and student affairs staff are to collaborate successfully to enhance student learning.

Figures 1, 2, and 3 illustrate the mental models of faculty, student affairs staff, and first-year, traditional-age students. These models are abstract representations of groups of people. They have not been empirically validated and are presented to stimulate discussions among faculty, staff, and students that can set the stage for the collaborative efforts necessary to create effective learning environments. Also, some individuals are not represented by the model for their group. For example, faculty may differ by discipline in terms of how they think about learning (Austin 1990; Kuh and Whitt 1988). More than one student model is needed to accommodate the many different types of students (e.g., full-time traditional-age senior students; 35-year-old students taking one class). By comparing the models side by side the differences become more obvious in the ways faculty, staff, and students think about what is important in undergraduate education and begin to explain why collaboration and communication are sometimes difficult even though people may have similar aspirations for their students.

Most people are unaware of their mental models and how they influence their behavior.

The items listed in the core of the models are most important to the respective group. The further from the core, the less important or valuable the activity. For example, faculty tend to focus on the curriculum and those programs and services that support classroom activities (figure 1) (L. Upcraft, personal communication, January 1995). The guiding assumption is that what matters in undergraduate education occurs primarily in the classroom. Student affairs staff tend to focus on programs and services that emphasize students' social welfare needs and foster psycho-social development (figure 2). A guiding assumption of this model is that the out-of-class experiences of students make considerable contributions to the desired outcomes of college.

Figure 3 suggests that students' concerns and interests

FIGURE 1

WHAT MATTERS IN UNDERGRADUATE EDUCATION FACULTY MENTAL MODEL

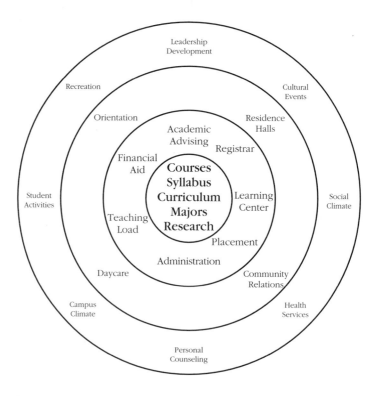

differ from those of the faculty and student affairs staff. Important to students are such matters as grades, making and keeping friends, being accepted by peers, obtaining the credentials to get a good job, and learning how to take care of themselves and manage their time. They tend to focus less on activities and services considered important by either faculty or student affairs staff unless they recognize a need for such services (figure 3).

Acknowledging the existence of different mental models, and the assumptions on which they are based, is a necessary step toward developing a shared language and institutional vision of what matters to student learning. Both a common language and a shared vision are essential if faculty and staff are to motivate students to apply what they are learning in

FIGURE 2

**WHAT MATTERS IN UNDERGRADUATE EDUCATION
STUDENT AFFAIRS MENTAL MODEL**

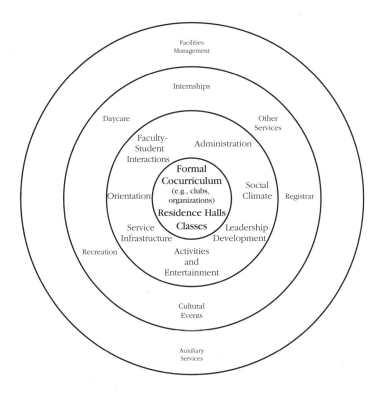

class to their lives beyond the classroom (and vice versa) and to get students to reflect on, and integrate, their classroom and out-of-class experiences. This means members of various groups must learn how members of other groups think and how to communicate more effectively with them. Faculty members, administrators, staff, and students also must develop a shared understanding of what connotes quality in undergraduate education, including its indices. Such indices may include measures of the learning climate, quality of teaching, student outcomes, and other factors that are essential to creating an ethos of learning throughout the campus.

FIGURE 3

WHAT MATTERS IN UNDERGRADUATE EDUCATION UNDERGRADUATE STUDENT (AGE 18-23) MENTAL MODEL

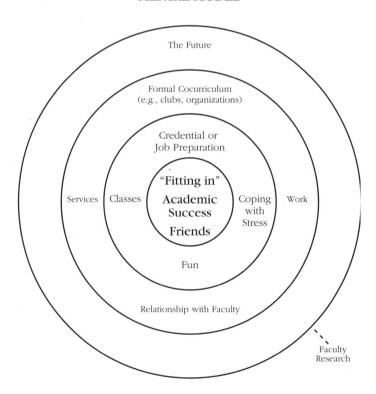

6. Attempt to shape the student culture in ways that will foster responsible behavior and valued outcomes of college

Using promising practices from the research on teaching and learning and developing a shared vision and collaborative working arrangements among faculty and staff are necessary but insufficient conditions for enhancing student learning. Even the most ambitious, elegantly designed institutional renewal strategy will fall short if the student culture is not addressed. The ability of institutional leaders to recognize and understand differences among individual students and student cultures seems to enhance their effectiveness in working with students and communicating desirable community standards.

Student culture exerts a significant influence on many aspects of college life including what a student learns because it determines the kinds of people with whom one spends time and the values and attitudes to which one is exposed (Baird 1988; Weidman 1984). When an institution allows students to determine the nature of social and academic relations, the influence of peers on student behavior increases (Wilson 1966). As a result, the expectations, attitudes, and values that characterize student cultures may or may not be congruent with those of the faculty. Indeed, there is evidence that at some colleges and universities the dominant student cultures have become estranged from the intellectual life of the institution (Horowitz 1987; Moffatt 1989.

For example, at some institutions students devote fewer than three hours per day outside of class to their studies (Marchese 1994; Wolf, Schmitz, and Ellis 1991). At the University of Missouri at Columbia, attendance at large lecture classes averages about 60 percent, a problem common to many other large universities (C. Schroeder, personal communication, February 21 1995). Students who join social fraternities are disadvantaged in terms of first-year gains in cognitive complexity (Pascarella, Edison, Whitt et al. In press) and humanitarianism (Pascarella, Edison, Nora et al. In press). These unequivocal findings coupled with the data that show that white male fraternity members engage in binge drinking to a greater extent than any other student group (Wechsler, personal communication, August 3 1995) make it clear that institutions should prohibit new students from joining such groups at least until after their first year of college.

Even institutions that attract large numbers of commuting students must contend with student cultures that may be antithetical to what the institution is trying to accomplish. For example, Weis (1985) found that the African American student culture at an urban community college essentially insured that the vast majority of African American students would return to squalid living conditions comparable to those from which they came. "It is the culture that students produce within the college that makes a significant contribution to low 'success' rates in traditional academic terms and the reproduction of a social structure that is strikingly unequal by class and race" (Weis 1985, p. 159).

Faculty and others can influence the student culture, at least indirectly. For example, faculty shape student behavior outside the classroom through their requirements for class and their interactions with students inside and outside the classroom. They also influence indirectly the nature of relations among students when they use lecture methods exclusively and require students to work independently (which tends to foster competition) or use a variety of techniques appropriate to the learning goals and setting such as active learning through small group work (which promotes cooperation).

Unless students are willing to work harder, and their peers endorse an expanded range of effort, attempts to increase learning productivity will meet with only limited success. A key factor, then, in enhancing institutional productivity and student learning is developing strategies that counter the conforming influence of the student culture that often dictates a low amount of effort be directed to academic activities (Hughes, Becker and Geer 1962; Kuh, In press).

Recommendations for Various Groups

At many institutions, student affairs professionals are held responsible for the quality of out-of-class living and learning environments. However, it is clear from the research on out-of-class learning experiences that all members of a college or university community contribute directly or indirectly to student involvement in educationally purposeful activities beyond the classroom. For this reason we begin with recommendations for those who tend to be less involved in promoting out-of-class learning but whose leadership and commitment are necessary to creating the type of seamless learning environments described in this report.

Governing boards

The expectations and responsibilities of governing boards depend to a great extent upon the traditions, context, and complexity of the institution. In most institutions they are expected to raise and steward institutional resources, appoint and evaluate the performance of institutional leaders, establish institutional goals and evaluate progress toward those goals, stimulate institutional renewal, and serve as a bridge as well as a buffer to the external environment (Taylor 1987). In carrying out these responsibilities, governing boards directly and indirectly influence student learning and personal development outside the classroom.

For example, governing boards approve the institution's formal mission statement. The board can make a strong statement about the importance of life outside the classroom by emphasizing undergraduate education and acknowledging the mutual shaping of in- and out-of-class experiences on student learning and personal development. Governing boards can have a positive influence on student life by providing strong, supportive statements about the importance of high-quality, out-of-class learning opportunities to attaining the institution's purposes and allocating resources to create and maintain such opportunities. Governing boards also influence student learning outside the classroom by approving policies ranging from library hours and the availability of technology, to the institution's position on diversity. Other board actions include encouraging (or discouraging) student participation in institutional governance structures (recall that students benefit in the areas of practical and interpersonal competence from such activities) and participating themselves in student-centered activities (e.g., new student convocations, commencement, mentoring programs, discussion groups on topics of importance to students).

On occasion, governing boards enact policies that have unintended negative consequences for out-of-class learning. For example, approving ancillary fee increases in order to offset shortfalls in tuition revenues may limit student access to programs and activities that were once an integral part of the undergraduate cocurricular collegiate experience.

Additional steps that governing boards can take to foster student learning outside the classroom include:

1. Requesting data on process indicators and outcomes that are consistent with the guidelines for assessment discussed previously in this report;
2. Asking for information from students directly about how they spend their time and what they gain from their experiences outside the classroom;
3. Challenging faculty leaders and staff to modify core functions and processes that will help create an ethos of learning throughout the institution; and
4. Hiring a president who values undergraduate education and who has high expectations for student, faculty, and staff performance, inside and outside the classroom.

President

As with captains of industry, the president with the support of governing board and cabinet members establish goals, priorities, and policies for the core activities in which their organization engages. These include among other things research, undergraduate and often graduate teaching, and service to the community. As the keeper of the institution's vision, the president is the symbolic leader for all institutional stakeholders. How, where, and to what ends the president spends time influence what members of the institution think is valued and worth doing—including the quality of student learning and development opportunities outside the classroom (Kuh et al. 1991). This suggests that the degree to which student learning outside the classroom will be valued by the institution is a function of the amount of attention the president gives to these issues when talking with the press, governing board, state legislators, and other groups. To be persuasive on these topics the president must have accurate information about students and their experiences.

In many cases, teaching, research, and service are the three primary missions of a college. The president should convey institutional priorities to the board, and have detailed plans that outline how specific goals and objectives will have an impact on student learning outside the classroom. This means the president must make it clear to the chief budget officer that academic goals lead budgetary expenditures, not vice versa.

Recognizing that different student cultures exist, the president should charge specific groups (e.g., fraternity advisers, minority student affairs staff) to monitor how institutional policies and practices mirror what the educational mission statement states as integral to the success of all its students. The contributions of certain groups (e.g., student affairs) to high-quality, out-of-class experiences are often invisible to the casual observer. Their important work is reflected in institutional safety nets and efforts to teach and support students to do—and learn—things for themselves. That this work often goes unnoticed by faculty and even students themselves does not mean that it should go unrecognized or unrewarded. A president who values out-of-class contributions frequently celebrates this work, not only through public kudos, but also by making sure that these people have a cabinet-level voice to influence institutional policy.

Other activities that presidents can undertake to promote student learning outside the classroom include:

1. Annually reminding the governing board and academic administrators about the value of out-of-class experiences to student goals and the institution's mission;
2. Talking with students on a regular basis in venues that acknowledge the importance of life outside the classroom;
3. Holding the student affairs unit accountable for articulating and responding to students' out-of-class needs (National Association of Student Personnel Administrators 1987); and
4. When appropriate, encouraging external stakeholders to support, morally and financially, out-of-class programs and services that serve educational purposes.

Academic administrators
The provost or senior academic officer is a key player in fostering a spirit of collaboration between academic and student affairs and in encouraging faculty to acknowledge the importance of life outside the classroom to achieving the institution's educational objectives and student's educational and personal goals. All too often, in-class and out-of-class learning are perceived as discrete and separate from the academic mission (Kuh, Shedd, and Whitt 1987). Various factors, such as changing faculty reward systems (Bowen

and Schuster 1986), encourage faculty members to isolate themselves from students out of class, contributing to the perception that academic and nonacademic aspects of students' lives are separable, with the former clearly more important than the latter.

Senior academic officers are in a strategic position to shape an institutional ethos that values learning outside the classroom. An important role is to teach new faculty, administrators, and staff about institutional values regarding student learning outside the classroom. By recommending that new student orientation include more intellectual activities (e.g., small group faculty- or staff-lead discussions of required summer readings) and encouraging students to become involved in departmental organizations, the academic dean sends powerful messages about what college is about and creates appropriate expectations for both new students and faculty. Department chairs can make new faculty members aware of the importance of out-of-class contacts with students to student satisfaction and persistence (Tinto 1993). What other messages can academic administrators send to faculty about involvement with students after class and the role of out-of-class learning opportunities in fulfilling the institutional mission?

To create those conditions under which student learning best occurs, academic administrators might consider:

1. Revising tenure and promotion policies in order to recognize faculty involvement with students in out-of-class settings (e.g., serving as advisers to student organizations, working with undergraduates on out-of-class projects);
2. Assessing the extent to which academic support services are meeting the needs of all students and are compatible with the institution's mission and philosophy;
3. Appointing faculty members to student life committees and student affairs staff to academic affairs committees and task forces;
4. Establishing strong communication links between academic and student affairs; and
5. Hiring learning-centered faculty members.

Faculty
Faculty probably have as much influence on out-of-class learning environments as any other group excluding stu-

dents themselves. This is because they determine in large part how much students study by the amount of academic work they assign and what learning resources in addition to the course text are needed to complete assignments (e.g., library, study groups). This is why learning-centered faculty are critical to creating seamless learning environments. Learning-centered faculty view undergraduates as active partners in learning rather than empty vessels to be filled. They exhibit an intellectual inquisitiveness that is contagious, thereby creating a sense of wonder and excitement in their students. They have high expectations for student performance, and challenge students to discover and use their intellectual and social capabilities by using the institution's resources for learning to full advantage (e.g., the library, cultural events, and work opportunities both on and off the campus). They recognize that, for most students, knowledge must be applied to be useful and relevant. For this reason, learning-centered faculty members design assignments and class projects that help students purposefully integrate in-class knowledge with their out-of-class lives (Kuh et al. 1991).

It is not surprising that such outcomes as academic skills are associated infrequently with out-of-class experiences, compared with other outcomes, such as autonomy and confidence. At the same time, it is disappointing that knowledge application is not often associated with out-of-class activities. Collegiate environments offer innumerable opportunities to use information obtained from many courses of study (e.g., political science, psychology, sociology) in dealing with the problems and challenges of daily life. Course assignments should encourage students to extend their understanding beyond the primary text and lectures, and require them to use campus learning resources—the library, the museum, the theater, convocations, and special lectures—by working them into class assignments. To encourage more knowledge application, faculty could structure assignments that require students to illustrate how they are using class material in other areas of their lives. For example, faculty can promote ways to address current institutional-societal issues in the curriculum (e.g., asking students in business courses to work on case studies addressing institutional financial issues or societal concerns about the financing of higher education). In an introductory philosophy course at Earlham College

Learning-centered faculty view undergraduates as active partners in learning rather than empty vessels to be filled.

focusing on sexual ethics, students are asked to locate several articles about affirmative action, annotate two that take different points of view, and relate them to their own ethical positions. "Another in U.S. History asks students to examine primary materials on slave life or the abolition . . . compare them with their text's treatment of the subjects, and to write their own brief accounts of the issues or events" (Erickson and Strommer 1991, p. 131). Such assignments encourage students to both prepare for class and to develop better library research skills, skills that can be used in other areas of life (e.g., how to find information on a specific topic).

Many of the pedagogical advantages that occur naturally in experiential learning to teach higher order learning skills can be artificially created in academic learning environments (Angelo and Cross 1993). In a course in family studies, an instructor devised an exercise to give students an opportunity to experience what it is like to be a primary caretaker. Each student was given an egg and told to "take care of it" and to return it in one piece at the next class. Those who did would receive extra credit. Students returned with a variety of experiences to share, which allowed students and the instructor to make concrete links to key points from the assigned readings on caretaking (Erickson and Strommer 1991).

By assigning cooperative learning tasks, faculty influence the student culture by asking students to work together after class (Goodsell, Maher, and Tinto 1992). For example, learning communities are attempts to restructure curriculum by linking courses around a common theme and enrolling students as a self-contained cohort group. In addition to taking classes together they are encouraged to connect explicitly ideas and disciplines. Such learning communities create a sense of group identity, cohesion, purpose, self-esteem, sensitivity and respect for others, and improved communication and writing skills. In addition, increases in persistence and achievement are linked with participation in learning communities (MacGregor 1993; Tinto 1994; Tinto, Russo, and Kadel 1994).

Requiring students to work together in groups that meet outside the classroom also helps create a psychological sense of community by intertwining out-of-class activities with an academic course and can contribute to feelings of support among participants. This support, in turn, allows faculty and staff to engage the participants in more challenging academic work and to set clear expectations for how students are to spend their time outside the classroom. In a study on the experiences of community college students, Okun, Sandler, and Baumann (1988) found that teachers' involvement with positive school events boosted the positive feelings associated with that event and increased students' satisfaction with the collegiate experience. Data from the Harvard Assessment Seminars suggest that students in study groups do better academically and are more engaged than students working either alone or in large groups (Light 1992). Such groups, when formed with diverse group members, may help reduce alienation for students of color and also enhance human understanding (Smith 1990).

In addition to using technology and individually paced learning, faculty might consider revising class assignments so that they are more relevant to students' lives and their learning goals while at the same time ensuring appropriate coverage of material and intellectual integrity. Instead of suggesting long term papers, which encourage plagiarism and support those who operate term paper companies, alternative methods of library research can be developed (Farber in Erickson and Strommer 1991).

Encouraging students to work together and to apply their learning beyond the classroom is not only beneficial for students (McKeachie et al. 1986), but it also pays off for faculty (Johnson, Johnson, and Smith 1991). Learning productivity increases since academic work is structured to extend beyond the classroom. In addition, cooperative learning tends to increase the beneficial relationships that form among faculty from various departments, across schools, and between academic and support divisions. By working with student affairs staff, for example, faculty can extend their ability to shape the learning environment well beyond the classroom (e.g., faculty in residence programs, integrating volunteer service with classroom activities). Organizational barriers start to break down, resulting in an institutional environment better able to meet the learning needs of students.

Class attendance requirements and policies warrant review. As mentioned earlier, when students do not go to class, or think that going to class is not important, this has a negative effect on the out-of-class environment in that students have too much free time on their hands. Moreover, the institution makes a statement about the relative importance of learning when it does not make it clear to students that class work is a high priority. At the same time, something must occur in class that makes it worth the student's time to participate. The use of active learning techniques and, equally important, connecting material covered in a course to life outside the classroom, is key.

Most important, faculty must challenge the norms that discourage meaningful contact between faculty and students beyond the classroom (Kuh 1991b). At many institutions, students and faculty seem to have struck an implicit bargain that says, in effect, "you leave me alone and I will leave you alone." For faculty, this "disengagement compact" has been encouraged by reward systems that favor research over teaching, by the increasing size of institutions, and by the status attainment phenomenon whereby teaching institutions attempt to become more like research universities (Kuh et al. 1991). The student side of the bargain is motivated by the fact that, for too many students, a meaningful college experience does not include development of the intellect or interaction with faculty. To be successful in this effort, faculty must become familiar with ways of encouraging students intellectually to examine their thinking and their relationships between thinking, feeling, and the practical competencies that must be integrated to develop the whole student. As Baxter Magolda (1992b) observed:

Until students feel that what they think has some validity, it is impossible for them to view themselves as capable of constructing knowledge. . . . Speaking in their own voice through class involvement, evaluation techniques, leadership opportunities, and peer interactions helped students come to see themselves as sources of knowledge (p. 376).

When talking with students, faculty should emphasize intellectual matters and course material. While some relaxed conversation may be necessary to develop rapport and trust, student learning seems to be enhanced when faculty members engage students intellectually and relate their in- and out-of-class experiences to the mission and educational purposes of the institution or to students' educational and vocational goals. "Students will be more likely to learn to think reflectively when this institutional goal is communicated in many institutional contexts, with multiple opportunities in both curricular and cocurricular settings to learn and practice thinking skills" (King and Kitchener 1994, p. 240).

The climate of the academic department is important (Feldman and Newcomb 1969; Jacobs 1986), especially for students at metropolitan institutions and community colleges whose primary contact with the institution is the classroom (Kuh, Vesper, and Krehbiel 1994). The major department represents an important social and intellectual subenvironment for the student when it encourages frequent contacts among peers with similar academic and career interests (Pascarella and Terenzini 1991).

Other suggestions for faculty include:

1. Designing methods to evaluate students' ability to integrate in-class and out-of-class experiences;
2. Making certain that students clearly understand what is expected of them with regard to using institutional resources for learning (e.g., the library, academic assistance center), the most effective ways to study, and expectations for the amount of time required for each class; and
3. Structuring assignments so that students must reflect on their out-of-class experiences, such as asking students to keep a 'learning log' of how class material is relevant their lives beyond the classroom.

Student affairs administrators

Many believe that student affairs staff play a key role in promoting student involvement in educationally purposeful activities beyond the classroom (American College Personnel Association 1994; Love 1995).

The increasing size of institutions and changing expectations for faculty suggest that student affairs staff on many campuses may play an increasingly prominent role. . . . Indeed, at some large institutions, student affairs staff have become the de facto *caretakers of the undergraduate experience. Along with a few other highly visible administrators and a shrinking number of student-centered faculty members, student affairs staff model how students should handle obligations, opportunities, and responsibili-*

ties in an academic community. Student affairs staff are more likely than faculty members to be present during the many "teachable" moments that occur out of the classroom and are in a better position to encourage students to take advantage of such moments (Kuh et al. 1991, p. 351).

As mentioned earlier, student affairs staff influence that fraction of undergraduates who actively participate in the formal, institutionally sponsored extracurriculum, such as student government and residence hall programs. However, fewer students today are involved in those activities.

The key task is for student affairs in partnership with the faculty to couple more tightly the connections between the curriculum and out-of-class life. This means that student affairs staff must understand their institution's mission and educational purposes and how the curriculum is organized to address these educational purposes. In addition, they must be able to describe how out-of-class environments and events complement the institutional mission and the learning goals of students. Student affairs staff must also be able to explain to faculty and others (students, parents) how life beyond the classroom can help faculty attain their instructional objectives and the institution's purposes. This means that student affairs must collect current data about students (e.g., characteristics, attitudes, needs, and activities) including the ways in which students spend their out-of-class time and share this information with the president, governing board, faculty, academic administrators, and the students themselves.

For this reason, student affairs staff must be knowledgeable about outcomes assessment, and should collaborate with assessment specialists and other agents to design ways for incorporating out-of-class experiences into comprehensive strategies to determine the impact of college. For example, studies that attempt to link various out-of-class experiences (e.g., voluntarism, student government, on-campus job) with specific outcomes would be useful to accrediting agencies for accountability purposes, and to institutional decision makers for program improvement purposes.

As illustrated earlier in the review of the literature, learning occurs in many different settings, both on and off the campus (e.g., residential units, library, the university center, classrooms, faculty offices, place of employment). To a substantial degree, the student culture determines what and how much students learn. Student affairs professionals have the most contact with students and should be knowledgeable about the various student subcultures and their influence on the institution's climates for learning. Student affairs professionals must use this knowledge to rethink the rationale and design of programs and services and to suggest ways they can more effectively document the impact of their efforts and the curriculum on students. This will require that student affairs staff examine their assumptions, expectations, goals, and philosophies with an eye toward expanding their portfolio of challenges and responsibilities to include high levels of student learning and academic achievement as well as personal development. Just as faculty set clear expectations with respect to student effort and performance in class so, too, should student affairs staff set expectations for student involvement and standards outside of class.

Student affairs staff must clarify what the institution values and translate the values into behavioral terms for life outside the classroom. For example, suppose an institution says (and really means) that its students: (a) must prepare for every class; (b) complete assignments in a timely fashion; and (c) participate fully in classroom activities (National Association of Student Personnel Administrators 1995). What is the role of student affairs in helping students meet these expectations? What can student affairs do in collaboration with faculty to encourage, cajole, and challenge students to devote the necessary time and energy to these tasks, acquire the skills they need to succeed academically, and help their peers to obtain resources (e.g., library materials)?

To maximize the benefits of life outside the classroom, student affairs professionals must use effective teaching approaches in their interactions with students and monitor who gets involved in what type of activities to be certain some students are not systematically excluded. Thus, student affairs professionals must be prepared to work with students from a variety of backgrounds. Personnel must be grounded in theory and research that offer insight into student learning and personal development and the influence of the environment on student performance and satisfaction. They must clarify expectations for students consistent with this knowledge base and organize activities so that students reflect on their experiences in thoughtful ways to attain the desired outcomes. In addition, they should employ active learning strategies, periodically assess the impact of their efforts on student performance, and offer timely feedback to students about their behavior under various circumstances.

Student affairs staff could promote more knowledge application by asking students on a regular basis to apply what they are learning in class to life outside the classroom. Consider the residence hall director who routinely invites students during casual conversation to share the three or four most important things they learned that week, or the student activities adviser who challenges student leaders to apply material from their political science, psychology, and communications classes to the work of their organizations. Such encounters teach students how to evaluate the reasoning they see and hear including their own. Students who take part in campus decision-making groups or programming boards should be challenged to reflect on the quality of their own judgments. Student government is another important venue through which students learn the skills necessary for effective citizenship. In order to make student government especially meaningful, student affairs staff should encourage student leaders to make connections between their government experiences and academic work, broader institutional and societal issues, and personal needs.

Student affairs staff at residential campuses may employ a number of techniques to create rich, engaging out-of-class environments focused on learning. Of course, living in a residence hall does not necessarily ensure that students will benefit in the desired ways. This is because residential environments can be either "isolating or stimulating and can promote academic achievement or rowdy escapism, depending on who the residents are and whether they partake of the growth opportunities around them" (Chickering and Reisser 1993, p. 400). To enhance their impact, residence halls should be organized to create a focused study environment (e.g., designated quiet floors, using academic tutors, grouping students by academic major, and designing living-learning centers) (Pascarella, Terenzini, and Blimling 1994). Housing arrangements may be structured to encourage students to engage with others who share common academic interests and majors, a passion for service activities, or common vocational interests. Small student groupings structured around common academic, service, and work interests help to break down student isolation and anonymity, and increase the likelihood of significant engagement in academic work that leads to gains in student learning.

Other ways to increase the chances that living in campus residences will have the desired impact include assigning roommates intentionally; using regulations, policies, and hall management procedures to foster development (e.g., community living contracts); remodeling or building new units that allow maximum participation and interaction; personalizing living spaces; and incorporating activities and experiences that are directly linked to academic experiences (e.g., faculty fellows programs, poetry readings, recitals) (Chickering and Reisser 1993; Kuh et al. 1991; Schroeder, Mable, and Associates 1994).

Creating human scale settings, irrespective of institutional size or physical barriers (e.g., lack of facilities that allow people to come together), is an important condition in which student affairs professionals have a significant influence. Large institutions and commuter institutions have a number of challenges in this regard.

Smaller communities of students form more easily for students living in residence halls. Commuter students also need to be given the opportunity to naturally become a part of small groups of students. Involvement in learning communities, or enrolling students as cohort groups in courses centered around a common theme, is one way to create an on-going, small-group environment for commuters (Chickering and Reisser 1993). In addition, institutional policies, practices, and expectations that encourage meaningful involvement (for example, required participation in service-learning activities, faculty requirements for small group discussions outside of class), clearly communicate that the institution values strong student interaction, irrespective of the lack of residence halls.

For older, part-time, commuter students, and those who may have family members to care for, student affairs staff can encourage students to become more engaged in their learning outside the class by fashioning programs and activities that recognize the multiple commitments of these students and include their significant others and family members in learning opportunities. This may be accomplished through designated events that offer child care, and developing an environment that is welcoming to students and their loved ones. Specific ideas include arranging weekend learning programs (for example, "How to Paint," "Science-Made-Fun) geared for students' children. While children are engaged in these weekend activities their student-parents can use the library, meet with academic advisers and counselors, or work with other students in study groups. Similar programs can be arranged to accommodate the schedules of spouses and significant others.

For traditional-age students, programs can be geared toward orienting parents to the institutional expectations for student involvement in the out-of-class environment. These programs would emphasize the rich potential of the out-of-class environment, provide parents with suggested questions with which to engage students in discussions about their learning through out-of-class experiences, and suggest possible out-of-class activities that seem to be particularly beneficial (e.g., study abroad programs, peer helper programs).

At commuter institutions opportunities for students to interact with one another outside classes are not plentiful for most students. Thus, student affairs staff must promote the establishment of gathering spaces for students, and support activities and programs to help students feel a part of the institutional community. Student unions and other gathering places are crucial to encourage commuter students to interact with faculty and peers. In addition, commuter institutions must clearly communicate to students the expectation that involvement in all aspects of the institutional environment is valued, encouraged, and supported.

Another approach for encouraging students at commuter institutions to get involved in institutional governance and other educationally purposeful activities is to designate a period of time (e.g., 11 A.M.-noon) one or two days a week during which classes are not scheduled. During this time, students can meet with study groups, engage in institutional and community service activities, and take advantage of other learning opportunities. Reserving this period to do the work of the institution may also encourage more faculty to take part in institutional governance (Kuh et al. 1991).

Even though small, residential campuses have some distinct advantages for creating human-scale environments (e.g., size, community-building traditions), they, too, have their challenges. The environment may be too homogeneous, stifling, or alienating for some students, so these institutions must also be intentional about the types of environments which they create. Student affairs staff should be sensitive to the need to balance small, supportive environments with academically challenging and culturally diverse environments. To help promote an awareness of differences and multiple perspectives student affairs staff could sponsor celebrations around designated awareness months (e.g., National Black History Month, National Women's History Month), and actively support a diverse student body. This means that out-of-class opportunities need to reflect different viewpoints, should be inclusive of different ethnic and racial groups, and should be designed to encourage optimum engagement, student effort, and growth. In addition, staff must ensure that all student organizations adhere to nonexclusionary or nonalienating membership policies so that diverse thought and perspectives may be shared, supported, or challenged.

The research suggests that intellectual development is—in part—a function of the quality of peer relations.

A number of other student affairs-sponsored programs and services can be used to encourage students to make the most of their learning opportunities. First-year programs, for example, can assist students in their transition to college by stressing involvement, adherence to academic standards, and the benefits of diverse environments. New students need to be aware that although being accepted by peers is important, it is equally important to establish a strong academic foundation. Thus, enhancing academic skills is critical in the first year of college and most institutions make available various programs for this purpose (e.g., study skills courses, cocurricular writing- and math-skills workshops).

The research suggests that intellectual development is—in part—a function of the quality of peer relations (Perry 1981; Astin 1993b). Because peer group influences are so strong, students should be asked to think about the people with whom they spend time. The types of environments that foster cooperative relationships must be identified. Students should be encouraged to think and talk about how their friends spend time (e.g., eating in the student union; studying in the library; participating in or attending theater, art, music, or recreational activities). Do people in their affinity group represent a wide range of views? How can students be encouraged to expand their network of peers (e.g., join orientation, residence hall, or peer advising staffs, participate in mentoring programs and community service projects)?

In addition to peers, students need to think about their relations with faculty and staff members. Students should be encouraged to seek out faculty members in out-of-class settings, to ask questions about topics discussed in classes, to volunteer to help on research projects, or to ask faculty members to become involved in a "faculty friends" program for residential or commuting students. Students who participate in out-of-class formal leadership experiences can ask faculty members to come talk with their student organizations or serve as an adviser for an activity. These conversations need not be limited to the topics faculty teach. However, such interactions are more likely to have a positive effect on learning if they focus on intellectual matters or vocational interests as contrasted with social pleasantries exclusively.

Counselors and advisers could devote some time with every student client to reflect on educational and life goals. Programs for specific populations (e.g., first-generation students, students with disabilities) offer support to those at greatest risk of dropping out. It is particularly important to direct specific attention to first-generation university students and teach them how to take advantage of learning resources (e.g., libraries, academic skills center), as these students often lack tacit knowledge about college and university life.

At some institutions it may be appropriate that students be required to participate in certain activities. For example, at a college with a strong social service ethos (e.g., Berea, Earlham), requiring students to engage in a designated number of activities with a service component is consistent with the educational mission. Such experiences can be particularly meaningful if students reflect with peers or others (e.g., student affairs staff) about the value of these experiences, or write about the experience in a "cornerstone" course to demonstrate fulfillment of the requirement.

Other suggestions for student affairs professionals include:

1. Becoming familiar with the institution's culture, mission, philosophy, history and traditions and their influence on students' use of out-of-class time;

2. Using the institution's mission and philosophy to test the appropriateness and necessity of programs and services;
3. Establishing strong communication links with academic administrators, faculty members, and student leaders; and
4. Making certain that an early warning system is in place and working for all students who face circumstances that may jeopardize their academic success (Kuh and Schuh 1991; Kuh et al. 1991).

Students

Few undergraduate students are likely to read this book. However, faculty, staff, parents, and others have numerous occasions to advise undergraduates about how to use their out-of-class time responsibly. Indeed, "student responsibility is an essential ingredient for student development" (Davis and Murrell 1993b, p. 3). In taking responsibility for their own learning and personal development, how can students use to educational advantage the human and physical resources a college or university makes available?

All students, including those who do not have the luxury of choosing among a variety of institutions, must learn how to use the resources of the institution that they are attending—and the amount of time and energy successful students invest in their studies and other activities. For students who can choose from among a number of institutions for under-graduate study, the first way they exercise responsibility is by selecting an institution that takes undergraduate educa-tion seriously. How committed is the institution to the undergraduate experience—and how is this commitment expressed in daily practices? Is the institution committed to the inclusion of a variety of people and ideas? Some of this information can be gleaned from institutional publications and college guide books (e.g., *Barron's, Peterson's Guide*). Visiting the institution is the single best way to answer these and other questions (Schuh and Kuh 1991).

One sign of whether an institution considers undergradu-ate students to be important is how often and for what pur-poses professors and students meet together informally, such as over a cup of coffee in the student union. Admissions staff and tour guides should inform prospective students about the accessibility of faculty members and the degree to which teaching is important to the faculty (Kuh

1991c). Although getting a job after graduation should not, in most cases, be the dominant factor in deciding where to go to college, the availability of off-campus internships and opportunities to work and study at the same time can be an important part of one's education (Schuh and Kuh 1991).

Prospective students also should have access to information about other kinds of educational programs that extend learning beyond the classroom and laboratory, such as guest lectures and off-campus or study abroad programs. They also should find out what is required to get involved in various organizations and activities. At some institutions, students are expected to be responsible for their learning and living activities, such as establishing quiet hours in residences and determining how their social funds should be spent. At others, faculty and staff take a more active role in students' lives. Even at the places where students are expected to be responsible, there are services that students can use when academic or personal concerns become overwhelming. Prospective students should know what types of assistance are available, and how helpful currently enrolled students consider these services (Schuh and Kuh 1991).

Students new to college need to realize they have a limited amount of time to take advantage of learning opportunities. In order to make informed decisions about how to invest their time and energy, students should participate actively in new student orientation programs (Schuh and Kuh 1991). Students also should fully explore the housing options at or near the institutions, including living-learning alternatives (e.g., academic theme houses) and consider enrolling in an honors course or participating in a cultural-exchange program (e.g., study abroad). These experiences are linked to gains in a variety of important outcome areas as reported earlier. Students seeking employment should first try to obtain work on campus that is related to their academic or cocurricular interests.

Commuter students can enroll in courses focused on a common theme that use cohort groups to foster continuing contact among the same students in two or more classes. Such experiences can provide many of the same opportunities as residential living-learning alternatives.

In order to increase involvement in the collegiate experience, students sometimes need to point out to faculty, staff, and other students those policies and practices that are imposing unnecessary limitations on their participation in opportunities—and be willing to engage in processes that may help alleviate such constraints. Is more affordable child care needed, or is child care needed during different time periods than what is currently available? If spouses, partners, or children of students are encouraged to participate, will this increase students' participation in certain kinds of cocurricular experiences? Are meetings of student organizations held at times in which a variety of students can participate? Are students who raise such concerns invited to participate in processes that might help broaden opportunities for learning and personal development?

Other suggestions for students include:

1. Enrolling in courses that employ active learning processes because these activities foster a wide variety of valuable academic and social skills;
2. Discussing with others (faculty, student affairs staff, peers) your educational goals, academic progress, and how classroom learning can be used in one's life outside the classroom and vice versa; and
3. Developing a portfolio of items showing the cocurricular activities in which you have participated and the benefits gained from these activities.

Other agents

Many other people also influence students' out-of-class learning experiences. These people include—but are not limited to—family members, clerical and custodial staff, and such external groups as accreditation agencies and employers, to name two. These groups directly influence student learning and development (e.g., family support, or lack of it, for obtaining the degree) or indirectly influence the institution's educational environment (e.g., accreditation agency requirements for assessing student learning). In any case, the role and impact of these other agents is real and any examination of the learning environment must account for them.

The role of parents and family members, especially for traditional-age students, has been fairly clear. Family members help to provide the emotional and financial support that enables individuals to expend energy on their education. Family members also can play a significant role in helping students understand the importance of their total educational experience. For example, parents can talk to their children about both in-class and out-of-class learning. Parents can work with students to help identify a healthy balance of learning experiences. In addition, they can help to emphasize institutional expectations for academic work and personal behavior. Simply having somebody to talk with can be a significant, positive contribution to creating a sense of belonging for some students.

The learning and personal development benefits to be realized by nontraditional students also are affected by their families. For many so-called nontraditional students, spouses, children, and parents provide the emotional and moral support necessary for them to persist in their studies. Spouses, in particular, can assist nontraditional students in making the transition from work, the military, or unemployment into the college environment by stressing the importance of becoming involved in all aspects of the institutional environment and, when appropriate, participating with their student in some of these activities.

Accreditation agencies now require information from institutions about student outcomes, understanding that the role of life outside the classroom to these outcomes is especially important. Even though many faculty, administrators, and staff consider accrediting requirements to be a nuisance, these agencies influence student learning through asking institutions to concentrate less on activities and resources, and more on outcomes and impact (Banta and Associates 1993). Accrediting agencies now require institutions to, at a minimum, show how programs and services contribute to the accomplishment of the institutional mission, and to develop ways in which to measure this impact (Ewell 1994).

Students cannot take full advantage of an institution's resources for learning if they perceive the environment to be unfriendly, unsafe, or unclean. For this reason custodial and clerical staff are also important in fostering learning and personal development. In order to make the desired contributions, staff must become knowledgeable about the benefits of out-of-class experiences for student learning, perhaps through staff development activities. Clerical and custodial staff can also be encouraged to participate in out-of-class experiences with students (such as building a Habitat for Humanity house) and should feel free to engage students in discussions on the impact of the experience. A caveat: student learning and personal development are not maximized when people do things for students (e.g., completing paperwork, making phone calls) that students can and must learn to do for themselves.

The Key Tasks

The single most important thing that institutional agents can do to enhance student learning is to get students to think more often about what they are doing—in classes and other areas of their lives—and to apply what they are learning to both. This means student affairs staff, faculty, and others must spend more time engaged with students, asking them to interpret and think about what they are learning, and to talk with peers and faculty about those experiences that are most important to their learning.

Reflection, the critical behavior, is not a natural act, especially for most first-year and second-year traditional-age students. Faculty and student affairs staff can foster reflective thinking by "adapting their responses to students' assumptions about knowledge" (King and Kitchener 1994, pp. 232-233). King and Kitchener provide examples of how student affairs staff can select strategies that are consistent with students who hold various sets of epistemic assumptions. Learning is most productive when students are encouraged to reflect on the lessons that come from real life experiences when solving real problems (Strange 1992). "For younger students without work experience, internships, cooperative education, and community service programs can be richer learning experiences than an equal amount of time spent in the classroom" (Cross 1993, p. 7). How can other types of experiences that frequently occur outside the classroom, both on and off the campus, be used to help students integrate and think about or reflect on what they are learning in class?

College life can be confusing for those who have not yet developed the capacity to reflect on and integrate their experiences. K. Patricia Cross (1994), professor emeritus at the University of California, Berkeley, explained how student affairs staff and faculty can help students make meaning of their experience. She likened the university experience to a jigsaw puzzle. Students go to classes and participate in various events and activities, inside and outside the classroom—daily, weekly, and throughout the academic year. These thousands of temporally independent experiences are represented by puzzle pieces. Too many students finish college with a bag of unconnected puzzle pieces, not a coherent picture of their experience. This is because, in part, they do not have the picture of the completed puzzle to compare against; that is they lack a visual image of what the college experience could or should look like—what they are creating with all these puzzle pieces. Certainly, the undergraduate experience cannot and should not look alike for all students. At the same time, however, without someone encouraging students to fit the pieces together to create in their mind's eye their own unique picture of what they would like university to be, too many students do not create a coherent, meaningful picture for themselves.

Need for Additional Research

There is more to discover about the contributions of out-of-class experiences to student learning and personal development. Unless the mutually shaping, interactive effects of classroom and out-of-class activities are taken into account, "the magnitudes of those effects will be underestimated and the relative importance of various general or specific aspects of the college experience will remain unclear (Terenzini, Springer, Pascarella, and Nora 1995, p. 40). Key questions to address in future research include:

1. What are the institutional conditions that encourage students to use out-of-class time in more educationally purposeful ways?
2. How are the learning and personal development outcomes related to these conditions?
3. How can institutions marshall their existing resources, including technology, to produce more learning by undergraduates?
4. How can we assess gains in student learning related to the out-of-class experience?
5. What can academic administrators, faculty, student affairs staff, students, and others do together to create the conditions that promote learning outside the classroom, including those beyond the campus, and connect their learning to the institution's academic goals?

A series of studies could be helpful of how students adapt their environments for social and academic purposes. Are enough areas of intellectual retreat suitable for reflection and small group interaction available at the institution in addition to libraries and residence hall rooms? Can cafeterias and other eating spaces be adapted when not in use for other purposes for discussions with students and faculty? Are enough niches and special gathering places available for students and faculty to come together? Can more be created? How much institutional space should be allocated for social and recreational purposes? And what is the balance of adaptable space in terms of its use for activities that complement the academic mission of the institution?

More research is needed on how to harness peer influence to further the educational aims of the institution, such as nurturing student cultures that foster a high level of student involvement in educationally purposeful activities (Kuh, In press). The teaching and learning context of the institution also needs to be evaluated when deciding where to focus effort to create developmentally powerful subenvironments, such as academic departments that draw students in with their own ethos of learning, theme-oriented residence halls, and so forth. At the same time, institutions are not monolithic organizations with a single uniform set of environmental stimuli impinging equally on all members. Instead, many subcultures exist on a college campus. They differentially affect people and their influence needs to be taken into account.

CONCLUSION

Institutional efforts must be directed to creating environments in which students will concentrate on their studies as well as collaborate with each other and faculty. The conditions that promote student learning outside the classroom cannot be created by any one individual—president, academic or student life dean, or governing board member. However, by working together, by linking programs and activities across the academic and out-of-class dimensions of campus life, and removing obstacles to students' pursuit of their academic and personal goals, an institution can enhance student learning, especially when its faculty, staff, and administrators know the conditions under which learning best occurs and work together to create those conditions.

Students change as whole, integrated persons during college as they engage in both academic and nonacademic activities in and outside the classroom (Pascarella and Terenzini 1991). Breadth of experiences in both intellectual and social activities is important to learning (Pace 1990), particularly when the academic, interpersonal, and out-of-class experiences are mutually supporting. In other words, it is a student's total level of engagement in various learning activities that is most important. Limiting involvement to any one portion of the collegiate experience, therefore, appears to reduce the amount and type of change a student might experience. The implications for policy and practice were summarized by Pascarella and Terenzini (1991):

> *Educational impact is enhanced when policy and programs "are broadly conceived and diverse. . . . Campuswide, single purpose programs rarely have the desired impact. Institutions are more productive when* all *their activities are compatible with the institutions's educational purposes"* (p. 655).

Faculty members signal the end of classes using various phrases: "class dismissed," "see you next week," or "that's all for today." Occasionally nothing is said. Although what is said (or not said) at the close of class varies, all-too-often the sentiment is the same. Faculty and students go their separate ways with students getting the message that their learning is suspended, off duty as it were, at least until the next scheduled 55-minute class meeting.

To enhance institutional productivity and greater levels of student learning and personal development, colleges and universities need to create an ethos that carries the message that inherent in every setting is the potential for learning—the biology lab, library, academic advisers' office, residence hall lounge, place of employment, student union, community service, and playing fields. The key task for all institutions—large or small, public or private, commuter or residential—is to motivate students to see college as a seamless web of learning opportunities, a time when "school is always in session and life challenges us to excel at being both enthusiastic student and inspired teacher" (Brown 1992, np). Institutions most likely to succeed in transcending the artificial boundaries between in-class and out-of-class experiences are those that value all their students, provide ample opportunities for them to participate in educationally-purposeful activities outside the classroom, and continuously ask students to reflect on how they are spending their time and how what they are learning in class can be used in out-of-class settings and vice versa.

REFERENCES

The Educational Resources Information Center (ERIC) Clearinghouse on Higher Education abstracts and indexes the current literature on higher education for inclusion in ERIC's data base and announcement in ERIC's monthly bibliogrpahic journal, *Resources in Education* (RIE). Most of these publications are available through the ERIC Document Reproduction Service (EDRS). For publications cited in this bibliography that are available from EDRS, ordering number and price code are included. Readers who wish to order a publication should write to the ERIC Document Reproduction Service, 7420 Fullerton Rd., Suite 110, Springfield, VA 22153-2852. (Phone orders with VISA or MasterCard are taken at 800-443-ERIC or 703-440-1400.) When ordering, please specify the document (ED) number. Documents are available as noted in microfiche (MF) and paper copy (PC). If you have the price code ready when you call EDRS, an exact price can be quoted. The last page of the latest issue of *Resources in Education* also has the current cost, listed by code.

Abrahamowicz, D. 1988. "College Involvement, Perceptions, and Satisfaction: A Study of Membership in Student Organizations." *Journal of College Student Development* 29(3): 233–38.

Adams, G., and S. Fitch. 1983. "Psychological Environments of University Departments: Effects on College Students' Identity Status and Ego Stage Development." *Journal of Personality and Social Psychology* 44(6): 1266–75.

Aitken, N.D. 1982. "College Student Performance, Satisfaction, and Retention." *Journal of Higher Education* 53(1): 32–50.

Aleman, A.M. 1994. "The Cognitive Value of College Women's Friendships." Paper presented at the annual meeting of the American Educational Research Association, April, New Orleans.

Alexander, L.T., R. Gur, and L. Patterson. 1974. "Peer-assisted Learning." *Improving Human Performance Quarterly* 3(4): 175–86.

Alexander, P.A., and P.K. Murphy. 1994. "The Research Base for APA's Learner-Centered Psychological Principles." Paper presented at the annual meeting of the American Educational Research Association, April, New Orleans.

Allen, W. 1987. "Black Colleges vs. White Colleges: The Fork in the Road for Black Students." *Change* 19(3): 28–34.

Almquist, E., and S. Angrist. 1970. "Career Salience and Atypicality of Occupational Choice Among College Women." *Journal of Marriage and the Family* 32(2): 242–48.

———. 1971. "Role Model Influences on College Women's Career Aspirations." *Merrill-Palmer Quarterly of Behavior & Development* 17(3): 263–79.

American Association of Higher Education. 1992. *Principles of*

Good Practice for Assessing Student Learning. Washington, D.C.: Author.

American College Personnel Association. 1994. *The Student Learning Imperative: Implications for Student Affairs.* Washington, D.C.: Author.

Anchors, S., K.B. Douglas, and M.K. Kasper. 1993. "Developing and Enhancing Student Communities." In *Student Housing and Residential Life: A Handbook for Professionals Committed to Student Development Goals,* edited by R.B. Winston Jr., S. Anchors, and Associates. San Francisco: Jossey-Bass.

Angelo, T.A., and K.P. Cross. 1993. *Classroom Assessment Techniques: A Handbook for College Teachers.* 2d ed. San Francisco: Jossey-Bass.

Annis, L. 1983. "The Processes and Effects of Peer Tutoring." *Human Learning* 2(1): 39–47.

Arnold, J., G. Kuh, N. Vesper, and J. Schuh. 1993. "Student Age and Enrollment Status as Determinants of Learning and Personal Development at Metropolitan Institutions." *Journal of College Student Development* 34(1): 11–16.

Arnold, K. 1987. "Values and Vocations: The Career Aspirations of Academically Gifted Females in the First Five Years After High School." Paper presented at the annual meeting of the American Educational Research Association, April, Washington, D.C.

Astin, A.W. 1973. "The Impact of Dormitory Living on Students." *Educational Record* 54(9): 204–10.

———. 1975. *Preventing Students from Dropping Out.* San Francisco: Jossey-Bass.

———. 1977. *Four Critical Years: The Effects of College on Beliefs, Attitudes, and Knowledge.* San Francisco: Jossey-Bass.

———. 1982. *Minorities in American Higher Education: Recent Trends, Current Prospects, and Recommendations.* San Francisco: Jossey-Bass.

———. 1984. "Student Involvement: A Developmental Theory for Higher Education." *Journal of College Student Personnel* 25(4): 297–308.

———. 1985. *Achieving Educational Excellence: A Critical Assessment of Priorities and Practices in Higher Education.* San Francisco: Jossey-Bass.

———. 1991. *Assessment for Excellence: The Philosophy and Practice of Assessment and Evaluation in Higher Education.* New York: American Council on Education/Macmillan Publishing Co.

———. 1993a. "Diversity and Multiculturalism on Campus: How are Students Affected?" *Change* 25(2): 44–49.

———. 1993b. *What Matters in College:* Four Critical Years *Revisited.* San Francisco: Jossey-Bass.

Astin, H., and L. Kent. 1983. "Gender Roles in Transition: Research and Policy Implications for Higher Education." *Journal of Higher Education* 54(3): 309–24.

Austin, A. 1990. "Faculty Cultures, Faculty Values." In *Assessing Academic Climates and Cultures, New Directions for Institutional Research,* edited by W.G. Tierney. No. 68. San Francisco: Jossey-Bass.

Baier, J.L., and E.G. Whipple. 1990. "Greek Values and Attitudes: A Comparison with Independents." *NASPA Journal* 28(1): 43–53.

Baird, L. 1988. "The College Environment Revisited: A Review of Research and Theory." In *Higher Education: Handbook of Theory and Research,* edited by J. Smart. Vol. 4. New York: Agathon Press.

Bandura, A. 1977. *Social Learning Theory.* Englewood Cliffs, N.J.: Prentice-Hall.

———. 1986. *Social Foundations of Thought and Action: A Social Cognitive Theory.* Englewood Cliffs, N.J.: Prentice-Hall.

Bank, B.J., R.L. Slavings, and B.J. Biddle. 1990. "Effects of Peer, Faculty, and Parental Influences on Students' Persistence." *Sociology of Education* 63(3): 208–25.

Banta, T.W. 1993. "Summary and Conclusion: Are We Making a Difference?" In *Making a Difference: Outcomes of a Decade of Assessment in Higher Education,* edited by T.W. Banta and Associates. San Francisco: Jossey-Bass.

Banta, T.W., and Associates. 1993. *Making a Difference: Outcomes of a Decade of Assessment in Higher Education.* San Francisco: Jossey-Bass.

Bargh, J.A., and Y. Schul. 1980. "On the Cognitive Benefits of Teaching." *Journal of Educational Psychology* 72(5): 593–604.

Baxter Magolda, M. 1992a. "Cocurricular Influences on College Students' Intellectual Development." *Journal of College Student Development* 33, 203–13.

———. 1992b. *Knowing and Reasoning in College: Gender Related Patterns in Students' Intellectual Development.* San Francisco: Jossey-Bass.

———. 1994. "Promoting Intellectual Development Through the Co-Curriculum." Paper presented at the meeting of the Association for the Study of Higher Education, November, Tucson, Ariz.

Bean, J.P. 1980. "Dropouts and Turnover: The Synthesis and Test of a Causal Model of Student Attrition." *Research in Higher Education* 12(2): 155–87.

———. 1985. "Interaction Effects Based on Class Level in an Exploratory Model of College Student Dropout Syndrome." *American Educational Research Journal* 22(1): 35–64.

Bean, J.P., and R. Bradley. 1986. "Untangling the Satisfaction-

Performance Relationship for College Students." *Journal of Higher Education* 57(4): 393–412.

Bean, J.P., and G.D. Kuh. 1984. "The Reciprocity Between Student-Faculty Informal Contact and the Undergraduate Grade Point Average of University Students." *Research in Higher Education* 21(4): 461–77.

Bean, J.P., and N. Vesper. 1994. "Gender Differences in College Student Satisfaction." Tucson: Paper presented at the annual meeting of the Association for the Study of Higher Education, November, Tucson, Ariz. ED 375 728. 33pp. MF–01; PC–02.

Belenky, M.F., B.M. Clinchy, N.R. Goldberg, and J.M. Tarule. 1986. *Women's Ways of Knowing: The Development of Self, Voice, and Mind*. New York: Basic Books.

Benjamin, E. 1993. "Assuring Access to Higher Education Requires Renewal, Not Restructuring." *Footnotes* 14(1): 4–5.

Benware, C., and E. Deci. 1984. "Quality of Learning with An Active Versus Passive Motivational Set." *American Educational Research Journal* 21(4): 755–65.

Berliner, D.C. 1984. "The Half-Full Glass: A Review of Research on Teaching." In *Using What We Know About Teaching.* edited by P.L. Hosford. Alexandria, Va.: Association for Supervision and Curriculum Development.

Bers, T.H., and K.E. Smith. 1991. "Persistence of Community College Students: The Influence of Student Intent and Academic and Social Integration." *Research in Higher Education* 32(5): 539–56.

Bertin, B., E. Ferrant, J. Whiteley, and N. Yokota. 1985. "Influences on Character Development During the College Years." In *Promoting Values Education in Student Development,* edited by J. Dalton. Washington, D.C.: National Association of Student Personnel Administrators.

Bisconti, A., and J. Kessler. 1980. *College and Other Stepping Stones: A Study of Learning Experiences that Contribute to Effective Performance in Early and Long-Running Jobs.* Bethlehem, Pa.: College Placement Council Foundation. ED 193 558. 101pp. MF–01; PC–05.

Blackwell, J. 1981. *Mainstreaming Outsiders: The Production of Black Professionals.* Bayside, N.Y.: General Hall.

Blimling, G. 1993. "The Influence of College Residence Halls on Students." In *Higher Education: Handbook of Theory and Research,* edited by J. Smart. Vol. 9. New York: Agathon Press.

Bowen, H.R. 1977. *Investment in Learning.* San Francisco: Jossey-Bass.

Bowen, H.R., and J.H. Schuster. 1986. *American Professors: A National Resource Imperiled.* New York: Oxford Univ. Press.

Boyer, E. 1987. *College: The Undergraduate Experience in America.*

New York: Harper & Row.

Braxton, J.m., and E. Brier. 1989. "Melding Organizational and Interactional Theories of Student Attrition: A Path Analytic Study." *Review of Higher Education* 13(1): 47–61.

Braxton, J.M., E.M. Brier, L. Herzog, and E. Pascarella. 1990. "Becoming a Lawyer: The Effects of College and College Experiences." *Review of Higher Education* 13(3): 285–302.

Brigman, S., G. Kuh, and S. Stager. 1982. "Those Who Choose to Leave: Why Students Voluntarily Withdraw from College." *Journal of the National Association of Women Deans, Administrators, and Counselors* 45(3): 3–8.

Brophy, J., and T. Good. 1974. *Teacher-Student Relationships: Causes and Consequences.* New York: Holt, Reinhart, and Winston.

Brower, A.M. 1992. "The 'Second Half' of Student Integration: The Effects of Life Task Predominance on Student Persistence." *Journal of Higher Education* 63(4): 441–62.

Brown, H.J., Jr. 1992. *Live and Learn and Pass It On.* Nashville, Tenn.: Rutledge Hill.

Brown, R., and D. DeCoster. 1982. *Mentoring-Transcript Systems for Promoting Student Growth.* San Francisco: Jossey-Bass.

Brown, R., J. Winkworth, and L. Braskamp. 1973. "Student Development in a Coed Residence Hall: Promiscuity, Prophylactic, or Panacea?" *Journal of College Student Personnel* 14(2): 98–104.

Bruffee, K.A. 1993. *Collaborative Learning: Higher Education, Interdependence, and the Authority of Knowledge.* Baltimore: The Johns Hopkins Univ. Press.

———. 1995. "Sharing Our Toys: Cooperative Learning Versus Collaborative Learning." *Change* 27(1):12–18.

Callan, P.M. 1995. "Forward." In *Preserving the Higher Education Legacy: A Conversation with California Leaders,* edited by J. Immerwahr (with J. Boese). San Jose: The California Higher Education Policy Center. ED 381 069. 25pp. MF–01; PC–01.

Calhoon, R., and A. Reddy. 1968. "The Frantic Search for Predictors of Success: 50 Years of Confusion and Contradiction." *Journal of College Placement* 28(3): 54–66.

Cappelli, P. 1992. "College, Students, and the Workplace: Assessing Performance to Improve the Fit." *Change* 24(6): 55–61.

Carnegie Foundation for the Advancement of Teaching. 1990. *Campus Life: In Search of Community.* Lawrenceville, N.J.: Princeton Univ. Press.

Carroll, J. 1988. "Freshman Retention and Attrition Factors at a Predominantly Black Urban Community College." *Journal of College Student Development* 29(1): 52–60.

Cashin, W.E. 1988. *Student Ratings of Teaching: A Summary of Research*. IDEA Paper No. 20. Manhattan: Center for Faculty Evaluation and Development, Kansas State Univ.

Cauble, M. 1976. "Formal Operations, Ego Identity, and Principled Morality: Are They Related?" *Developmental Psychology* 12(4): 363–64.

Center for the Study of the College Fraternity. 1982. *Survey of Fraternity Advisors*. Bloomington: Indiana Univ.

———. 1992. *Survey of Fraternity Advisors*. Bloomington: Indiana Univ.

Chickering, A.W. 1974. *Commuting Versus Resident Students: Overcoming Educational Inequalities of Living Off Campus*. San Francisco: Jossey-Bass.

Chickering, A.W., and Z.F. Gamson. 1987. "Seven Principles for Good Practice in Undergraduate Education." *AAHE Bulletin* 39(7): 3–7.

Chickering, A.W., and L. Reisser. 1993. *Education and Identity*. 2d ed. San Francisco: Jossey-Bass.

Christensen, C.R. 1987. *Teaching and the Case Method: Texts, Cases, and Readings*. Boston: Harvard Business School.

Christie, N., and S. Dinham. 1991. "Institutional and External Influences on Social Integration in the Freshman Year." *Journal of Higher Education* 62(4): 412–36.

Clewell, B., and M. Ficklen. 1986. *Improving Minority Retention in Higher Education: A Search for Effective Institutional Practices*. Princeton, N.J.: Educational Testing Service.

Cross, K.P. 1987. "Teaching for Learning." *AAHE Bulletin* 39(8): 3–7.

Cross, K.P. 1993. "Enhancing the Productivity of Learning: Reaction." *AAHE Bulletin* 46(4): 7–8.

Cross, K.P. 1994. "Response to Keynote Address." National Symposium on Student Learning, September, Bowling Green, Ohio.

Cross, K.P., and H. Astin. 1981. "Factors Influencing Black Students' Persistence in College." In *Black Students in Higher Education*, edited by G. Thomas. Westport, Conn.: Greenwood Press.

Davis, T., and P. Murrell. 1993a. "A Structural Model of Perceived Academic, Personal, and Vocational Gains Related to College Student Responsibility." *Research in Higher Education* 34(3): 267–89.

Davis, T., and P. Murrell. 1993b. *Turning Teaching into Learning: The Role of Student Responsibility in the Collegiate Experience*. ASHE-ERIC Higher Education Report No. 8. Washington, D.C.: The George Washington Univ., School of Education and Human Development. ED 372 703. 122pp. MF–01; PC–05

Deppe, M. 1989. "The Impact of Racial Diversity and Involvement on College Students' Social Concern Values." Paper presented at the annual meeting of the Association for the Study of Higher Education, November, Atlanta. ED 313 982. 53pp. MF–01; PC–03.

DuBois, P. 1978. "Participation in Sports and Occupational Attainment: A Comparative Study." *Research Quarterly* 49(1): 28–37.

Dunphy, L., T. Miller, T. Woodruff, and J. Nelson. 1987. "Exemplary Retention Strategies for the Freshman Year." In *Increasing Retention: Academic and Student Affairs Administrators in Partnership,* edited by M. Stodt and W. Klepper. New Directions in Higher Education, No. 60. San Francisco: Jossey-Bass.

Edgerton, R. 1993. "The New Public Mood and What It Means for Higher Education: A Conversation with Daniel Yankelovich." *AAHE Bulletin* 45(10): 3–7.

Edmonds, G. 1984. "Needs Assessment Strategy for Black Students: An Examination of Stressors and Program Implications." *Journal of Non-White Concerns in Personnel and Guidance.* 12(2): 48–56.

Education Commission of the States. 1994. *Quality Counts: Setting Expectations for Higher Education . . . and Making Them Count.* Denver: Author. ED 375 788. 13pp. MF–01; PC–01.

Ehrenberg, R., and D. Sherman. 1987. "Employment While in College, Academic Achievement, and Postcollege Outcomes: A Summary of Results." *Journal of Human Resources* 22(1): 1–23.

El-Khawas, E. 1980. "Differences in Academic Development During College." In *Men and Women Learning Together. A Study of College Students in the Late 70s.* Report of the Brown Project. Providence, R.I.: Brown Univ.

———. 1994. *Campus Trends 1994: A Time of Redirection.* Washington, D.C.: American Council on Education.

Endo, J., and R. Harpel. 1982. "The Effect of Student-Faculty Interaction on Students' Educational Outcomes." *Research in Higher Education* 16(2): 115–38.

———. 1983. "Student-Faculty Interaction and Its Effect on Freshman Year Outcomes at a Major State University." Paper presented at the Association for Institutional Research Forum, May, Toronto, Canada.

Erickson, B.L., and D.W. Strommer. 1991. *Teaching College Freshmen.* San Francisco: Jossey-Bass.

Erwin, T.D., and U. Delworth. 1982. "Formulating Environmental Constructs that Affect Students' Identity." *NASPA Journal* 20(1):47–55.

Ethington, C. 1994. "Institutional Effects on Educational Attainment: A Multi-Level Analysis." Paper presented at the meeting of the American Educational Research Association, April, New Orleans.

Ethington, C., and J. Smart. 1986. "Persistence to Graduate Education." *Research in Higher Education* 24(3): 287–303.

Ethington, C., J. Smart, and E. Pascarella. 1988. "Influences on Women's Entry Into Male-Dominated Occupations." *Higher Education* 17(5): 545–62.

Evanoski, P. 1988. "An Assessment of the Impact of Helping on the Helper for College Students." *College Student Journal* 22(1): 2–6.

Ewell, P.T. 1994. "Restoring Our Links with Society: The Neglected Art of Collective Responsibility." *Metropolitan Universities* 5(1): 79–87.

Ewell, P.T., and D.P. Jones. 1993. "Actions Matter: The Case for Indirect Measures in Assessing Higher Education's Progress on the National Education Goals." *Journal of General Education* 42(2): 123–48.

Faust, D., and J. Arbuthnot. 1978. "Relationship Between Moral and Piagetian reasoning and the Effectiveness of Moral Education." *Developmental Psychology* 14(4): 435–36.

Feldman, K.A. 1976. "The Superior College Teacher from the Students' View." *Research in Higher Education* 5(3): 243–88.

Feldman, K.A., and T. Newcomb. 1969. *The Impact of College on Students*. San Francisco: Jossey-Bass.

Fidler, P., and M. Hunter. 1989. "How Seminars Enhance Student Success." In *The Freshman Year Experience: Helping Students Survive and Succeed in College*, edited by M. Upcraft, J. Gardner, and Associates. San Francisco: Jossey-Bass.

Fincher, C. 1985. "Learning Theory and Research." In *Higher Education: Handbook of Theory and Research*, edited by J.C. Smart. Vol. 1. New York: Agathon Press.

Fleming, J. 1982. "Sex Differences in the Impact of College Environments on Black Students." In *The Undergraduate Woman: Issues in Educational Equity.* edited by P. Perun. Lexington, Mass.: D.C. Heath.

———. 1984. *Blacks in College: A Comparative Study of Students' Success in Black and White Institutions*. San Francisco: Jossey-Bass.

Forrest, A. 1985. "Creating Conditions for Student and Institutional Success." In *Increasing Student Retention: Effective Programs and Practices for Reducing the Dropout Rate*, edited by L. Noel, D. Levitz, and D. Saluri. San Francisco: Jossey-Bass.

Friedlander, J. 1980. *The Importance of Quality of Effort in Predicting College Student Attainment*. Los Angeles: Univ. of California.

Frisz, R.H. 1984. "The Perceived Influence of a Peer Advisement Program on a Group of Its Former Peer Advisors." *Personnel and Guidance Journal* 62(10): 616–19.

Frost, S.H. 1991. "Fostering the Critical Thinking of College Women

Through Academic Advising and Faculty Contact." *Journal of College Student Development* 32(4): 359–66.

Gaff, J.G. 1973. "Making a Difference: The Impacts of Faculty." *Journal of Higher Education* 44(8): 605–22.

Gardner, J.W. 1990. *On Leadership.* New York: The Free Press.

Gielow, C. R., and V. E. Lee. 1988. "The Effect of Institutional Characteristics on Student Satisfaction with College." Paper presented at the meeting of the American Educational Research Association, April, New Orleans.

Gilligan, C. 1982. *In a Different Voice: Psychological Theory and Women's Development.* Cambridge: Harvard Univ. Press.

Goldschmid, B., and M.L. Goldschmid. 1976. "Peer Teaching in Higher Education: A Review." *Higher Education* 4(1): 9–33.

Goldwhite, H. 1994. "Governance and Program Discontinuance in the California State University. *AAUP Footnotes* 15(1): 3.

Goodsell, A., M. Maher, and V. Tinto, eds. 1992. *Collaborative Learning: A Sourcebook for Higher Education.* University Park: National Center on Postsecondary Teaching, Learning and Assessment, The Pennsylvania State Univ. ED 357 705. 175pp. MF–01; PC–07.

Grosset, J.M. 1991. "Patterns of Integration, Commitment, and Student Characteristics and Retention Among Younger and Older Students." *Research in Higher Education* 32(2): 159–78.

Gurin, P., and E. Epps. 1975. *Black Consciousness, Identity and Achievement: A Study of Students in Historically Black Colleges.* New York: Wiley.

Hanks, M, and B. Eckland. 1976. "Athletics and Social Participation in the Educational Attainment Process." *Sociology of Education* 49(4): 271–94.

Hearn, J. 1987. "Impacts of Undergraduate Experiences on Aspirations and Plans for Graduate and Professional Education." *Research in Higher Education* 27(2): 119–41.

Hedlund, D.E., and J.T. Jones. 1970. "Effect of Student Personnel Services on Completion Rate in Two-Year Colleges." *Journal of College Student Personnel* 11(3): 196–99.

Henry, M., and H. Renaud. 1972. "Examined and Unexamined Lives." *Research Reporter* 7(1): 5–8.

Hill, B.A. 1994. "The Nature of Liberal Education Today." In *America's Investment in Liberal Education,* edited by D.H. Finifter and A.M. Hauptman. New Direction for Higher Education, No. 85. San Francisco: Jossey-Bass.

Holland, A., and M. Huba. 1989. "Psychosocial Development Among Student Paraprofessionals in a College Orientation Program." *Journal of College Student Development* 30(2): 100–105.

————. 1991. "Satisfaction with College among Participants in a Campus Service Program." *NASPA Journal* 28(4): 342–47.

Hood, A.A. 1984. "Student Development: Does Participation Affect Growth?" *Bulletin of the Association of College Unions-International* 54(6): 16–19.

Horowitz, H.L. 1987. *Campus Life: Undergraduate Cultures from the End of the Eighteenth Century to the Present.* New York: Knopf.

House, E. 1994. "Policy and Productivity in Higher Education. *Educational Researcher* 23(5): 27–32.

Howard, A. 1986. "College Experiences and Managerial Performance." *Journal of Applied Psychology Monographs* 71(3): 530–52.

Huebner, L.A. 1989. "Interaction of Student and Campus." In *Student Services: A Handbook for the Profession,* edited by U. Delworth and G. Hanson. San Francisco: Jossey-Bass.

Hughes, E., H. Becker, and B. Greer. 1962. "Student Culture and Academic Effort." In *The American College,* edited by N. Sanford. New York: Wiley.

Hunt, S. 1963. "Income Determinants for College Graduates and the Return to Educational Investment." *Yale Economic Essays* 3(2): 305–57.

Jacobs, J.A. 1986. "The Sex-aggregation of Fields of Study: Trends During the College Years." *Journal of Higher Education* 57(2): 134–54.

Jepsen, V. 1951. "Scholastic Proficiency and Vocational Success." *Educational and Psychological Measurement* 11(4): 616–28.

Johnson, D.W., R. Johnson, and K.A. Smith. 1991. *Cooperative Learning: Increasing College Faculty Instructional Productivity.* ASHE-ERIC Higher Education Report No. 4. Washington, D.C.: The George Washington Univ., School of Education and Human Development. ED 343 465. 168pp. MF–01; PC–07.

Johnstone, D.B. 1993. "Learning Productivity: A New Imperative for Higher Education." *Studies in Public Higher Education,* No. 3. Albany: State Univ. of New York, Office of the Chancellor.

Jussim, L. 1986. "Self-Fulfilling Prophecies: A Theoretical and Integrative Review." *Psychological Review* 93(4): 429–45.

Karman, F. 1973. "Women: Personal and Environmental Factors in Career Choice." Paper presented at the annual meeting of the American Educational Research Association, February, New Orleans. ED 074 400. 20pp. MF–01; PC–01.

Katz, J. 1974. "Coeducational Living: Effects upon Male-Female Relationships." In *Student Development and Education in College Residence Halls.* edited by D. DeCoster and P. Mable. Washington, D.C.: American College Personnel Association.

Kauffmann, N., and G.D. Kuh. 1985. "The Impact of Study Abroad on Personal Development of College Students." *Journal of International Student Personnel* 2(2): 6–10.

Keeton, M.T. 1971. *Shared Authority on Campus.* Washington, D.C.: American Association for Higher Education.

Kilgannon, S., and T. Erwin. 1992. "A Longitudinal Study About the Identity and Moral Development of Greek Students." *Journal of College Student Development* 33(3): 253–59.

Kilmann, R.H. 1984. *Beyond the Quick Fix: Managing Five Tracks to Organizational Success.* San Francisco: Jossey-Bass.

King, P.M., and K.S. Kitchener. 1994. *Developing Reflective Judgment.* San Francisco: Jossey-Bass.

King, S. 1973. *Five Lives at Harvard: Personality Change During College.* Cambridge, Mass.: Harvard Univ. Press.

Knox, W., P. Lindsay, and M. Kolb. 1992. "Higher Education, College Characteristics, and Student Experiences." *Journal of Higher Education* 63(3): 303–28.

———. 1993. *Does College Make a Difference? Long-Term Changes in Activities and Attitudes.* Westport, Conn.: Greenwood Press.

Komarovsky, M. 1985. *Women in College: Shaping New Feminine Identities.* New York: Basic Books.

Kowalski, C. 1977. *The Impact of College on Persisting and Nonpersisting Students.* New York: Philosophical Library.

Kuh, G.D. 1981. *Indices of Quality in the Undergraduate Experience.* AAHE-ERIC/Higher Education Research Report No. 4. Washington, D.C.: American Association for Higher Education. ED 213 340. 50pp. MF–01; PC–02.

———. 1991a. "Characteristics of Involving Colleges." In *The Role and Contributions of Student Affairs in Involving Colleges,* edited by G.D. Kuh and J. Schuh. Washington, D.C.: National Association of Student Personnel Administrators.

———. 1991b. "Teaching and Learning—After Class." *Journal on Excellence in College Teaching* 2: 35–51.

———. 1991c. "The Role of Admissions and Orientation in Creating Expectations for College Life." *College and University,* 66(2): 75–82.

———. 1993a. "In Their Own Words: What Students Learn Outside the Classroom." *American Educational Research Journal* 30(2): 277–304.

———. 1993b. "Ethos: Its Influence on Student Learning." *Liberal Education* 79(4): 22–31.

———. 1993c. "Assessing Campus Environments." In *Handbook of Student Affairs Administration,* edited by M. Barr. San Francisco: National Association of Student Personnel Administrators/Jossey-Bass.

———. 1995. "The Other Curriculum: Out-of-Class Experiences

Associated with Student Learning and Personal Development." *Journal of Higher Education* 66:(2) 123–55.

———. N.d. "Cultivating High Stakes Student Culture Research." *Research in Higher Education.* In press.

Kuh, G.D., and J.P. Lund. 1994. "What Students Gain from Participating in Student Government." In *Developing Student Government Leadership*, edited by M.C. Terrell and M.J. Cuyjet. New Directions for Student Services, No. 66. San Francisco: Jossey-Bass.

Kuh, G.D., and J. Schuh. 1991. "Conclusions and Recommendations." In *The Role and Contributions of Student Affairs in Involving Colleges,* edited by G.D. Kuh and J. Schuh. Washington, D.C.: National Association of Student Personnel Administrators.

Kuh, G.D., J. Schuh, E. Whitt, and Associates. 1991. *Involving Colleges: Successful Approaches to Fostering Student Learning and Development Outside the Classroom.* San Francisco: Jossey-Bass.

Kuh, G.D., J. Shedd, and E. Whitt. 1987. "Student Affairs and Liberal Education: Unrecognized (and Unappreciated) Common Law Partners." *Journal of College Student Personnel* 28(3): 252–60.

Kuh, G.D., N. Vesper, and L. Krehbiel. 1994. "Student Learning at Metropolitan Universities." In *Higher Education: Handbook of Theory and Research,* edited by J. Smart. Vol. 10. New York: Agathon Press.

Kuh, G.D., N. Vesper, and C.R. Pace. 1995. "Using Process Indicators to Estimate Student Gains Associated with Good Practices in Undergraduate Education." Paper presented at the meeting of the Association for the Study of Higher Education, November, Orlando.

Kuh, G.D., and E. Whitt. 1988. *The Invisible Tapestry: Culture in American Colleges and Universities.* ASHE-ERIC Higher Education Research Report No. 1. Washington, D.C.: Association for the Study of Higher Education. ED 299 934. 160 pp. PC–07; MF–01.

Kulik, C.C., J.A. Kulik, and P.A. Cohen. 1980. "Instructional Technology and College Teaching." *Teaching of Psychology* 7(4): 199–205.

Lacy, W. 1978. "Interpersonal Relationships as Mediators of Structural Effects: College Student Socialization in a Traditional and an Experimental University Environment." *Sociology of Education* 51(3): 201–11.

Lenning, O., ed. 1976. *Improving Educational Outcomes.* San Francisco: Jossey-Bass.

Lenning, O., P. Beal, and K. Sauer. 1980. *Retention and Attrition:*

Evidence for Action and Research. Boulder, Colo.: National Center for Higher Education Management Systems.

Lewin, K. 1936. *Principles of Topological Psychology*. New York: McGraw-Hill.

Light, R. 1990. *The Harvard Assessment Seminars: Explorations with Students and Faculty About Teaching, Learning, and Student Life*. Cambridge, Mass.: Harvard Univ. Graduate School of Education and Kennedy School of Government.

———. 1992. *The Harvard Assessment Seminars: Explorations with Students and Faculty about Teaching, Learning, and Student Life*. 2d report. Cambridge, Mass.: Harvard Univ. Graduate School of Education and Kennedy School of Government.

Lippmann, W. 1984. "The Indispensable Opposition." In *The Borzoi College Reader*, edited by C. Muscatine and M. Griffith. New York: Knopf.

Livingston, M., and M. Stewart. 1987. "Minority Students on a White Campus: Perception Is Truth." *NASPA Journal* 24(3): 39–49.

Loo, C., and G. Rolison. 1986. "Alienation of Ethnic Minority Students at a Predominantly White University." *Journal of Higher Education* 57(1): 58–77.

Love, P. 1995. "Exploring the Impact of Student Affairs Professionals on Student Outcomes." *Journal of College Student Development* 36(2): 162–70.

MacGregor, J., ed. 1993. *Student Self-Evaluation: Fostering Reflective Learning*. New Directions for Teaching and Learning. No. 56. San Francisco: Jossey-Bass.

McHale, M.T. 1994. "The Impact of College on Students' Attitudes Toward Women's Roles." Paper presented at the annual meeting of the Association for the Study of Higher Education, November, Tucson, Ariz. ED 375 711. 27pp. MF–01; PC–02.

MacKay, K.A., and Kuh, G.D. 1994. "A Comparison of Student Effort and Educational Gains of Caucasian and African-American Students at Predominantly White Colleges and Universities." *Journal of College Student Development* 35(3): 217–23.

McKeachie, W.J., P.R. Pintrich, Y. Lin, and D. Smith. 1986. *Teaching and Learning in the College Classroom: A Review of the Research Literature*. Ann Arbor: National Center for Research to Improve Postsecondary Teaching and Learning, Univ. of Michigan. ED 314 999. 124pp. MF–01; PC–05.

Madison, P. 1969. *Personality Development in College*. Reading, Mass.: Addison-Wesley.

Mallinckrodt, B. 1988. "Student Retention, Social Support, and Dropout Intention: Comparison of Black and White Students." *Journal of College Student Development* 29(1): 60–64.

Mallinckrodt, B., and W.E. Sedlacek. 1987. "Student Retention and Use of Campus Facilities by Race." *NASPA Journal* 24(3): 28–32.

Marchese, T. 1994. "Assessment." Address to the meeting of the American College Personnel Association, March, Indianapolis, Ind.

Marlowe, A.F., and C.D. Auvenshine. 1982. "Greek Membership: Its Impact on Moral Development of College Freshmen." *Journal of College Student Personnel* 23(1): 53–57.

Marsh, H.W. 1984. "Student's Evaluations of University Teaching: Dimensionality, Reliability, Validity, Potential Biases, and Utility." *Journal of Educational Psychology* 76(5): 707–54.

Menges, R.J., and B.C. Mathis.1988. *Key Resources on Teaching, Learning, Curriculum, and Faculty Development: A Guide to the Higher Education Literature.* San Francisco: Jossey-Bass.

Metzner, B. 1989. "Perceived Quality of Academic Advising: The Effect on Freshman Attrition." *American Educational Research Journal* 26(3): 422–42.

Micek, S., A. Service, and Y. Lee. 1975. *Outcome Measures and Procedures Manual.* Boulder, Colo.: National Center for Higher Education Management Systems, Western Interstate Commission on Higher Education.

Milem, J. 1994. "Attitude Changes in College students: Examining the Effect of College Peer Groups and Faculty Normative Groups." Paper presented at the meeting of the Association for the Study of Higher Education, November, Tucson, Ariz.

Moffatt, M. 1989. *Coming of Age in New Jersey: College and American Culture.* New Brunswick, N.J.: Rutgers Univ. Press.

Molla, B., and F. Westbrook. 1990. *White Student Attitudes about African American Students in a University Setting.* Research Report #9-90. College Park: Univ. of Maryland, Counseling Center. ED 328 164. 26pp. MF–01; PC–02.

Monteiro, L. 1980. "The College Academic Environment: Student Faculty Interaction." In *Men and Women Learning Together: A Study of College Students in the Late 70s.* Report of the Brown Project. Providence, R.I.: Brown Univ.

Murray, H.G. 1985. "Classroom Teaching Behaviors Related to College Teaching Effectiveness." In *Using Research to Improve Teaching,* edited by J.G. Donald and A.M. Sullivan. New Directions for Teaching and Learning, No. 23. San Fransisco: Jossey-Bass.

National Association of Student Personnel Administrators. 1987. *A Perspective on Student Affairs.* Washington, D.C: Author.

———. 1995. *Reasonable Expectations.* Washington, D.C.: Author.

National Center for Higher Education Management Systems. 1993. *A Preliminary Study of the Feasibility and Utility for National Policy of Instructional "Good Practice" Indicators in Undergraduate Education.* Boulder, Colo.: Author. ED 372 718. 68pp. MF–01; PC–03.

Nelson, R., T. Scott, and W. Bryan. 1984. "Precollege Characteristics and Early College Experiences as Predictors of Freshman Year Persistence." *Journal of College Student Personnel* 25(1): 50–54.

Nettles, M., A. Thoeny, and E. Gosman. 1986. "Comparative and Predictive Analyses of Black and White Students' College Achievement and Experience." *Journal of Higher Education* 57(3): 289–318.

Newcomb, T., D. Brown, J. Kulik, D. Reimer, and W. Revelle. 1971. "The University of Michigan's Residential College." In *The New Colleges: Toward an Appraisal,* edited by P. Dressel. Iowa City: American College Testing Program and American Association for Higher Education.

Newman, P.R., and B.M. Newman. 1978. "Identity Formation and the College Experience." *Adolescence* 13(50): 311–26.

Noddings, N. 1992. *The Challenge to Care in Schools: An Alternative Approach to Education.* New York: Teachers College Press.

Nora, A., L. Hagedorn, A. Cabrera, and E. Pacarella. 1994. "Differential Impacts of Academic and Social Experiences on College-Related Behavioral Outcomes Across Different Ethnic and Gender Groups at Four-Year Institutions." Paper presented at the meeting of the American Educational Research Association, April, New Orleans.

Nora, A., and L.I. Rendon. 1990. "Determinants of Predisposition to Transfer Among Community College Students: A Structural Model." *Research in Higher Education* 31(3): 235–55.

Okun, M., I. Sandler, and D. Baumann. 1988. "Buffer and Booster Effects as Event-Support Transactions." *American Journal of Community Psychology in Education* 16(3): 435–49.

Ory, J., and L. Braskamp. 1988. "Involvement and Growth of Students in Three Academic Programs." *Research in Higher Education* 28(2): 116–29.

Pace, C.R. 1979. *Measuring Outcomes of College: Fifty Years of Findings and Recommendations for the Future.* San Francisco: Jossey-Bass.

———. 1980. "Measuring the Quality of Student Effort." *Current Issues in Higher Education* (2): 10–16.

———. 1984. *Measuring the Quality of College Student Experiences.* Los Angeles: Univ. of California–Los Angeles, Center for the Study of Evaluation. ED 255 099. 142 pp. MF–01; PC not available EDRS.

———. 1987. *Good Things Go Together.* Los Angeles: Univ. of California–Los Angeles, Center for the Study of Evaluation.

———. 1990. *The Undergraduates: A Report of Their Activities and Progress in College in the 1980s.* Los Angeles: Univ. of California–Los Angeles, Center for the Study of Evaluation.

————. 1995. "From Good Practices to Good Products: Relating Good Practices in Undergraduate Education to Student Achievement." Paper presented at the meeting of the Association for Institutional Research, May, Boston.

Palmer, P.J. 1987. "Community, Conflict, and Ways of Knowing: Ways to Deepen Our Educational Agenda." *Change* 19(5): 20–25.

Parker, J., and J. Schmidt. 1982. "Effects of College Experience." In *Encyclopedia of Educational Research,* edited by H. Mitzel. 5th ed. New York: The Free Press.

Pascarella, E.T. 1980. "Student-Faculty Informal Contact and College Outcomes." *Review of Educational Research* 50(4): 545–95.

————. 1984. "Reassessing the Effects of Living On-Campus Versus Commuting to College: A Causal Modeling Approach." *Review of Higher Education* 7:(3) 247–60.

————. 1985. "Students' Affective Development Within the College Environment." *Journal of Higher Education* 56(6): 640–63.

Pascarella, E.T., L. Bohr, A. Nora, M. Desler, and B. Zusman. 1994. "Impacts of On-campus and Off-campus Work on First Year Cognitive Outcomes." *Journal of College Student Development* 35(5): 364–70.

Pascarella, E.T., L. Bohr, A. Nora, and P.T. Terenzini. 1995. "Intercollegiate Athletic Participation and Freshman-Year Cognitive Outcomes." *Journal of Higher Education* 66(4): 369–87.

Pascarella, E.T., L. Bohr, A. Nora, B. Zusman, P. Inman, and M. Desler. 1993. "Cognitive Impacts of Living on Campus Versus Commuting to College." *Journal of College Student Development* 34(3): 216–20.

Pascarella, E.T., and D.W. Chapman. 1983. "A Multi-Institutional, Path Analytic Validation of Tinto's Model of College Withdrawal." *American Educational Research Journal* 20(1): 87–102.

Pascarella, E.T., P. Duby, P.T. Terenzini, and B. Iverson. 1983. "Student-Faculty Relationships and Freshman Year Intellectual and Personal Growth in a Nonresidential Setting." *Journal of College Student Personnel* 24(5): 395–402.

Pascarella, E.,T. M. Edison, A. Nora, L. Hagedorn, and P.T. Terenzini. N.d.a. "Influences on Students' Openness to Diversity and Challenge in the First Year of College." *Journal of Higher Education.* In press.

Pascarella, E.T., M. Edison, E. Whitt, A. Nora, L. Hagedorn, and P.T. Terenzini. N.d.b. "Cognitive Effects of Greek Afilliation During the First Year of College." *NASPA Journal.* In press.

Pascarella, E.T., C. Ethington, and J. Smart. 1988. "The Influence of College on Humanitarian/Civic Involvement Values." *Journal of*

Higher Education 59(4): 412–37.

Pascarella, E.,T. and J. Smart. 1991. "Impact of Intercollegiate Athletic Participation for African American and Caucasian Men: Some Further Evidence." *Journal of College Student Development* 32: 123–30.

Pascarella, E.T., J. Smart, and C. Ethington. 1986. "Long-Term Persistence of Two-Year College Students." *Research in Higher Education* 24(1): 47–71.

Pascarella, E.T., J. Smart, C. Ethington, and M. Nettles. 1987. "The Influence of College on Self-Concept: A Consideration of Race and Gender Differences." *American Educational Research Journal* 24(1): 49–77.

Pascarella, E.T., and P.T. Terenzini. 1976. "Informal Interaction with Faculty and Freshman Ratings of Academic and Nonacademic Experience of College." *Journal of Educational Research* 70(1): 35–41.

———. 1977. "Patterns of Student-Faculty Informal Interaction Beyond the Classroom and Voluntary Freshman Attrition." *Journal of Higher Education* 48(5): 540–52.

———. 1979. "Interaction Effects in Spady's and Tinto's Conceptual Models of College Dropout." *Sociology of Education* 52(4): 197–210.

———. 1980. "Student-Faculty and Student-Peer Relationships as Mediators of the Structural Effects of Undergraduate Residence Arrangement." *Journal of Educational Research* 2(73): 344–53.

———. 1983. "Predicting Voluntary Freshman Year Persistence/Withdrawal Behavior in a Residential University: A Path Analytic Validation of Tinto's Model." *Journal of Educational Psychology* 75(2): 215–26.

———. 1991. *How College Affects Students: Findings and Insights from Twenty Years of Research*. San Francisco: Jossey-Bass.

Pascarella, E.T., P.T. Terenzini, and G. Blimling. 1994. "The Impact of Residential Life on Students." In *Realizing the Educational Potential of Residence Halls*, edited by C. Schroeder, P. Mable, and Associates. San Francisco: Jossey-Bass.

Perry, W.G., Jr. 1970. *Forms of Intellectual and Ethical Development in the College Years: A Scheme*. New York: Holt, Rinehart & Winston.

———. 1981. "Cognitive and Ethical Growth: The Making of Meaning." In *The Modern American College,* edited by A.W. Chickering and Associates. San Francisco: Jossey-Bass.

Pervin, L.A. 1968. "The College as a Social System: Student Perceptions of Students, Faculty, and Administration." *Journal of Educational Research* 61(6): 281–84.

Pike, G.R. 1991. "The Effects of Background, Coursework, and Involvement on Students' Grades and Satisfaction." *Research in*

Higher Education 32(1): 15–30.

————. 1993. "The Relationship Between Perceived Learning and Satisfaction with College: An Alternative View. *Research in Higher Education* 34(1): 23–40.

Pike, G.R., and J.W. Askew. 1990. "The Impact of Fraternity or Sorority Membership on Academic Involvement and Learning Outcomes." *NASPA Journal* 28(1):13–19.

Pounds, A. 1987. "Black Students' Needs on Predominantly White Campuses." In *Responding to the Needs of Today's Minority Students,* edited by M. Barr and M. L. Upcraft. New Directions for Student Services, No. 38. San Francisco: Jossey-Bass.

Pratt, C., and G. McLaughlin. 1989. "An Analysis of Predictors of College Students' Ethical Inclinations." *Research in Higher Education* 30(2): 195–219.

Reid, E. 1974. "Effects of Co-Residential Living on the Attitudes, Self-Image, and Role Expectations of College Women." *American Journal of Psychiatry* 131(5): 551–54.

Renninger, K.A., S. Hidi, and A. Krapp. 1992. *The Role of Interest in Learning and Development.* Hillsdale, N.J.: Erlbaum.

Robertson, J.A. 1980. "Black Student Satisfaction in the Deep South." *Journal of College Student Personnel* 21(6): 510–13.

Rowe, I., and J. Marcia. 1980. "Ego Identity Status, Formal Operations, and Moral Development." *Journal of Youth and Adolescence* 9(2): 87–99.

Russel, J., and R. Skinkle. 1990. "Evaluation of Peer-Adviser Effectiveness." *Journal of College Student Development* 31(5): 388–94.

Sanders, C.E. 1990. "Moral Reasoning of Male Freshmen." *Journal of College Student Development* 31(1): 5–8.

Sanford, N. 1962. *The American College.* New York: Wiley.

Schlossberg, N., A. Lynch, and A. Chickering. 1989. *Improving Higher Education Environments for Adults: Responsive Programs and Services from Entry to Departure.* San Francisco: Jossey-Bass.

Schroeder, C.C., P. Mable, and Associates. 1994. *Realizing the Educational Potential of Residence Halls.* San Francisco: Jossey-Bass.

Schuh, J., and G.D. Kuh. 1991. "Evaluating the Quality of Collegiate Environments." *Journal of College Admission* Winter: 17–22.

Schuh, J., and M. Laverty. 1983. "The Perceived Long-Term Influence of Holding a Significant Student Leadership Position." *Journal of College Student Personnel* 24(1): 28–32.

Senge, P.M. 1990. *The Fifth Discipline: The Art and Practice of the Learning Organization.* New York: Doubleday.

Serow, R.C., and J.I. Dreyden. 1990. "Community Service Among

College and University Students: Individual and Institutional Relationships." *Adolescence* 25(99): 553–66.

Shor, I. 1992. *Empowering Education: Critical Teaching for Social Change.* Chicago: Univ. of Chicago Press.

Simpson, C., K. Baker, and G. Mellinger. 1980. "Conventional Failures and Unconventional Dropouts: Comparing Different Types of University Withdrawals." *Sociology of Education* 53(4): 203–14.

Smart, J., and E. Pascarella. 1986. "Self-concept Development and Educational Degree Attainment." *Higher Education* 15(1–2): 3–15.

Smith, B.L., and J.T. MacGregor. 1992. "What is Collaborative Learning?" In *Collaborative Learning: A Sourcebook for Higher Education,* edited by A.S. Goodsell et al. University Park, Pa.: National Center on Postsecondary Teaching, Learning, & Assessment.

Smith, D. 1988. "Women's Colleges and Coed Colleges: Is There a Difference for Women?" *Journal of Higher Education* 61(2): 181–97.

———. 1990. "Embracing Diversity as a Central Campus Goal. *Academe* 76(6): 29–33.

Smith, K.A., D.W. Johnson, and R.T. Johnson. 1992. "Cooperative Learning and Positive Change in Higher Education." In *Collaborative Learning: A Sourcebook for Higher Education,* edited by A.S. Goodsell et al. University Park, Pa.: National Center on Postsecondary Teaching, Learning, & Assessment.

Sorcinelli, M.D. 1991. "Research Findings on the Seven Principles." In *Applying the Seven Principles for Good Practice in Undergraduate Education.,* edited by A.W. Chickering and Z.F. Gamson. New Directions for Teaching and Learning, No. 47. San Francisco: Jossey-Bass.

Spady, W. 1970. "Dropouts from Higher Education: An Interdisciplinary Review and Synthesis." *Interchange* 1(1): 64–85.

Springer, L., P. Terenzini, E. Pascarella, and A. Nora. 1995. "Influences on College Students' Orientations Toward Learning for Self-Understanding." *Journal of College Student Development* 36(1): 5–18.

Stern, G.G. 1970. *People in Context: Measuring Person-Environment Congruence in Education and Industry.* New York: Wiley.

Stoecker, J., and E.T. Pascarella. 1991. "Women's Colleges and Women's Career Attainments Revisited." *Journal of Higher Education* 62(4): 394–406.

Stoecker, J., E.T. Pascarella, and L. Wolfle. 1988. "Persistence in Higher Education: A Nine-Year Test of a Theoretical Model."

Journal of College Student Development 29(3): 196–209.

Strange, C.C. 1992. "Beyond the Classroom: Encouraging Reflective Thinking." *Liberal Education,* 78(1), 28–32.

Study Group on the Conditions of Excellence in American Higher Education. 1984. *Involvement in Learning: Realizing the Potential of American Higher Education.* Washington, D.C.: U. S. Department of Education. ED 246 833. 127pp. MF–01; PC–06.

Suczek, R. 1972. *The Best Laid Plans.* San Francisco: Jossey-Bass.

Suen, H. 1983. "Alienation and Attrition of Black College Students on a Predominantly White Campus." *Journal of College Student Personnel* 24(2): 117–21.

Taylor, B. 1987. *Working Effectively with Trustees: Building Cooperative Campus Leadership.* ASHE-ERIC Higher Education Report No. 2. Washington, D.C.: Association for the Study of Higher Education. ED 284 509. 141pp. MF–01; PC–06.

Taylor, W. 1982. "A Five-Year Attrition Study of an Undergraduate Class at the University of Tennessee at Chattanooga." *Dissertation Abstracts International* 43: 695A.

Terenzini, P.T., and E.T. Pascarella. 1980. "Student/Faculty Relationships and Freshman Year Educational Outcomes: A Further Investigation." *Journal of College Student Personnel* 21(6): 521–28.

———. 1994. "Living with Myths: Undergraduate Education in America." *Change* 26(1): 28–32.

Terenzini, P.T., L. Springer, E.T. Pascarella, and A. Nora. 1994. "The Multiple Influences of College on Students' Critical Thinking Skills." Paper presented at the annual meeting of the Association for the Study of Higher Education, November, Tucson, Ariz.

Terenzini, P.T., L. Springer, E.T. Pascarella, and A. Nora. 1995. "In and Out-of-Class Influences Affecting the Development of Students' Intellectual Orientations." *Review of Higher Education* 19(1): 23–44.

Terenzini, P.T., L. Springer, E.T. Pascarella, and A. Nora. N.d. "Influences Affecting the Development of Students' Critical Thinking Skills." *Research in Higher Education.* In press.

Terenzini, P.T., and T. Wright. 1987. "Influences on Students' Academic Growth During Four Years of College." *Research in Higher Education* 26(2): 161–79.

Thompson, J., V. Samiratedu, and J. Rafter. 1993. "The Effects of On-campus Residence on First-time College Students," *NASPA Journal* 31(1): 41–47.

Tidball, M.E. 1980. "Women's Colleges and Women Achievers Revisited." *Signs: Journal of Women in Culture and Society* 5(3): 504–17.

———. 1986. "Baccalaureate Origins of Recent Natural Science Doctorates." *Journal of Higher Education* 57(6): 606–20.

Tidball, M.E., and V. Kistiakowsky. 1976. "Baccalaureate Origins of American Scientists and Scholars." *Science* 196(4254): 646–52.

Tinto, V. 1975. "Dropout from Higher Education: A Theoretical Synthesis of Recent Research." *Review of Educational Research* 45(1): 89–125.

———. 1987. *Leaving College: Rethinking the Causes and Cures of Student Attrition*. Chicago: Univ. of Chicago Press.

———. 1993. *Leaving College: Rethinking the Causes and Cures of Student Attrition*. 2nd ed. Chicago: Univ. of Chicago Press.

———. 1994. *Building Learning Communities for New College Students*. University Park, Pa.: National Center on Postsecondary Teaching, Learning, and Assessment.

Tinto, V., P. Russo, and S. Kadel. 1994. "Constructing Educational Communities: Increasing Retention in Challenging Circumstances. *Community College Journal* 64(4): 26–30.

"To Dance With Change." 1994. *Policy Perspectives* 5(3): A1–12.

Treisman, U. 1992. "Studying Students Studying Calculus: A Look at the Lives of Minority Mathematics Students in College." *College Mathematics Journal* 23(5): 362–72.

Tucker, R.W. 1995. "Revisiting the Role of Higher Education in Workplace Competence." *Adult Assessment Forum* Spring: 3–5, 10, 14.

Vera, A.H., and H.A. Simon. 1993. "Situated Action: A Symbolic Interpretation." *Cognitive Science* 17(1): 7–48.

Vincow, G. 10 February 1993. *Pursuing the Vision of a Student-Centered Research University: A Progress Report to the Faculty*. Syracuse, N.Y.: Syracuse Univ., Office of the Vice Chancellor for Academic Affairs.

Volker, J. 1979. *Moral Reasoning and College Experience*. Higher Education and Cognitive-Social Development Project, Report No. 4. Minneapolis: Univ. of Minnesota.

Volkwein, J., M. King, and P. Terenzini. 1986. "Student-Faculty Relationships and Intellectual Growth Among Transfer Students." *Journal of Higher Education* 57(4): 413–30.

Voorhees, R.A. 1987. "Toward Building Models of Community College Persistence: A Logit Analysis." *Research in Higher Education* 26(2): 115–29.

Waldo, M. 1989. "Primary Prevention in University Residence Halls: Paraprofessional-led Relationship Enhancement Groups for College Roommates." *Journal of Counseling and Development* 67(8): 465–71.

Wallace, W. 1963. *Peer Groups and Student Achievement: The College Campus and Its Students*. Chicago: Univ. of Chicago, National Opinion Research Center.

Wallace, W. 1967. "Faculty and Fraternities: Organizational Influences on Student Achievement." *Administrative Science*

Quarterly 1(11): 643–70.

Walters, R., and D. Bray. 1963. "Today's Search for Tomorrow's Leaders." *Journal of College Placement* 24(1): 22–23.

Weidman, J. 1984. "Impacts of Campus Experiences and Parental Socialization on Undergraduates' Career Choices." *Research in Higher Education* 20(4): 445–76.

Weis, L. 1985. *Between Two Worlds: Black Students in an Urban Community College.* Boston: Routledge & Kegan Paul.

Wilder, D.H., A.E. Hoyt, B.S. Surbeck, J.C. Wilder, and P.I. Carney. 1986. "Greek Affiliation and Attitude Change in College Students." *Journal of College Student Development* 27(6): 510–19.

Whiteley, J. 1980. "A Developmental Intervention in Higher Education." In *Developmental Counseling and Teaching,* edited by V. Erickson and J. Whiteley. Pacific Grove, Calif.: Brooks/Cole.

Whiteley, J., and N. Yokota. 1988. *The Freshman Year Experience. Character Development in the Freshman Year and Over Four Years of Undergraduate Study.* Columbia: Univ. of South Carolina , Center for the Study of the Freshman Year Experience. ED 318 323. 44 pp. MF–01; PC–02.

Whitt, E.J. 1994. "Encouraging Adult Learner Involvement." *NASPA Journal* 31(4): 309–18.

Williamson, D.R., and D.G. Creamer. 1988. "Student Attrition in 2- and 4-Year Colleges: Application of a Theoretical Model." *Journal of College Student Development* 29(3): 210–17.

Willie, C., and D. Cunnigen. 1981. "Black Students in Higher Education: A Review of Studies, 1965-1980." In *Annual Review of Sociology,* edited by R. Turner and J. Short.Vol. 7. Palo Alto, Calif.: Annual Reviews.

Wilson, E.K. 1966. "The Entering Student: Attributes and Agents of Change." In *College Peer Groups,* edited by T. Newcomb and E. Wilson. Chicago: Aldine.

Wilson, L.S. 1992. "Beyond Conservation and Liberation: The Education of Our Aspirations." Thirteenth David Dodds Henry Lecture, February, Univ. of Illinois, Urbana-Champaign.

Wilson, R., J. Gaff, R. Dienst, L. Wood, and J. Bavry. 1975. *College Professors and Their Impact on Students.* New York: Wiley-Interscience.

Wilson, R., L. Wood, and J. Gaff. 1974. "Social-Psychological Accessibility and Faculty-Student Interaction Beyond the Classroom." *Sociology of Education* 47(1): 74–92.

Wingspread Group on Higher Education. 1993. *An American Imperative: Higher Expectations for Higher Education.* Racine, Wis.: Johnson Foundation.

Winter, D., D. McClelland, and A. Stewart. 1981. *A New Case for the Liberal Arts: Assessing Institutional Goals and Student*

Development. San Francisco: Jossey-Bass.

Wolf, B., T. Schmitz, and M. Ellis. 1991. *How Students Study: Views from Bloomington Campus Undergraduates.* Bloomington: Indiana Univ., Office for Academic Affairs and Dean of Faculties.

Wolfe, J.S. 1993. "Institutional Integration, Academic Success, and Persistence of First-Year Commuter and Resident Students." *Journal of College Student Development* 34(5): 321–26.

Wood, L., and R.C. Wilson. 1972. "Teachers with Impact." *Research Reporter* 7(2): 1–4.

INDEX

A

academic administrators, ways to foster student learning outside of classroom by, 78

Accreditation agencies, ways to foster student learning outside of classroom by, 94

active learning techniques, importance of, 82

advising programs

    correlated with higher graduation rates, 23

    inconsistent effects on persistence of students, 23

    must emphasize educational planning and skills needed to fill student goals, 68

African American students

    effect of involvement in activities of males, 40–41

    effect of social involvement on educational attainment, 15

    gains in cognitive complexity from out-of-class activities, 26

    interaction on campus unrelated to educational aspirations, 21

    leadership activities important for self esteem of males, 37

    strategies to increase mathematical and problem-solving talents, 50

    student culture insures that students return to squalid living conditions, 74

Aleman (1994), 45

American Association of Higher Education's Assessment Forum, 55

assessment of institutional practices and student performance principles, 55–56

Astin (1984), five postulates of involvement of, 12

Astin (1993a), 34

Astin (1993b), 23, 34, 44

    longitudinal study of 25,000 undergraduate students, 11

B

Bean and Vesper (1994), 19

Belenky, Clinchy, Goldberg, and Tarule (1986), 20

Braxton et al. (1990), 40

Bruffee (1993), 6

C

Center for Research and development in Higher Education, xii

Chickering and Reisser (1993), 58

Christie and Dinham (1991), 22

CIRP. See Cooperative Institutional Research Program

clerical and custodial staff, ways to foster student learning outside of classroom by, 94

cocurricular activities

more important for students with less commitment to attaining educational goals, 18

participation positively related to persistence, 17

cognitive complexity, 24

gains in out-of-class antecedents distributed across five areas, 26

positive correlation with quality of relations between students and faculty, 27

cognitive development, many dimensions have a social or interpersonal base, 31

collaborative learning, 53

college

as a time when "school is always in session...," 100

residence is most consistent determinant in shaping experience of , 43

College Student Experience Questionnaire, 11, 38, 68

Activity Scales, 28

College Student Satisfaction Questionnaire, 20

commuter institutions, promotion of student interaction outside of class within, 88

competence, interpersonal and intrapersonal 24–25

Cooperative Institutional Research Program, 11

data of, 34, 37

cooperative learning, 53

cooperative learning tasks, faculty influence through assigning, 80

"the craft of interdependence," 6

Cross (1994), 95

CSEQ. See College Student Experience Questionnaire

CSSQ. See College Student Satisfaction Questionnaire

curricular goals, importance of process indicators for,   56

D

development differences between on-campus and off-campus students, 38

Deppe (1989), 34

"disengagement compact," 82

diverse campus community, institutional commitment to educational benefits of, 64

DuBois (1978), 41

E

Earlham College, 79

educational attainment, categories of findings from research into, 13

educational impact, means for programs to have , 99

educationally purposeful activities, factors that foster engagement in, 58

employment part-time on campus positive correlation with educational attainment, 17

enhancing institutional productivity, need for, 2–3

environmental disorientation problem of minority students, 50

"ethic of care," 59

"ethic of membership," 59

Ethington (1994), 17

Ethington and Smart (1986), 18

ethos, role of institution's, 60–61

ethos of learning, need to cultivate, 64–65

Evanoski (1988), 36

expectations, importance for student performance, 51–52

F

faculty

liberal attitudes promotes student egalitarian attitude toward women, 37

ways to foster student learning outside of classroom by, 83

family members, ways to foster student learning outside of classroom by, 93–94

Female friendships as models for peer-assisted learning, 45

Fleming (1982, 1984), 29

foreign-language ability not associated with hours studying or doing homework, 31

Forest (1985), 23

fraternities

institutions should prohibit new students from joining in first year, 73–74

membership positively related to persistence, 21

"functional silos," 63

G

Gilligan (1982), 20

governing boards, ways to foster student learning outside of classroom by, 76

Graduate Record Examination. See GRE.

GRE, out of class activities negatively related to Verbal scores, 32
Grosset (1991), 20
Gurin and Epps (1975), 21

H

Hanks and Eckland (1976), 17
Harvard Assessment Seminars, 81
Harvard University, examination of teaching and learning at, 52
Hedlund and Jones (1970), 23
Hefferlin, J. B. Lon (1971), xii
high expectations result in greater student course satisfaction, 52
high school diploma is no longer enough to qualify for a well-
        paying job, 1
Hispanic students, strategies to increase mathematical and problem-
        solving talents, 50
holistic view of student learning, learning outside classroom most
        likely with, 49
Holland and Huba (1989), 34
Holland and Huba (1991), 20
Howard (1986), 40, 41
Humanitarianism, 24
        contributions of out-of-class activities to, 33–34
        effect of living environments on, 35
        effect of student-faculty contact on, 34
Hunt (1963), 41

I

informal student groups, importance of out-of-class activities of, 57
in loco parentis doctrine, effect of demise of, 66–67
institution's philosophy, definition of, 48–49
intellectual development
        as a function of peer relations quality, 89
        significantly related to amount of academic and
        interpersonal experiences, 29
Involvement in activities
        five postulates of, 12
        link to career-development and vocational success, 40–41
        positive effect for women, 40, 41
        principle, 12

J

Johnstone, D. Bruce (1993), xi
        popular image of widespread university shirking or

misplaced priorities is wrong, 4

K
King and Kitchener (1994), 95
knowledge acquisition and application, 24, 30
Kuh (1993a), 24, 42
Kuh (1995), 26, 27, 32, 37, 41, 42
Kuh et al. (1991), 38, 58
Kuh, Schuh, Whitt and Associates (1991), xiii

L
Leadership activities and self esteem, 36–37
learning and personal development outcomes, typology of, 24
"learning log," 83
learning theory and research in the tradition of psychology, 11–12
Light (1990, 1992), 52
Lippmann (1984), 61
living-learning center program, 38
living mission of a college or university, definition of, 47–48
living on campus, positive academic effect more apparent than
        real, 16–17
low expectations almost always deleterious, 52

M
McHale (1994), 37
Magolda (1992b), 27, 82
Measure of Epistemological Reflection, 27
men, major and career certainty are significant factors for, 20
mental models, 69
        importance of difference in core of faculty and students,
        70–72
Milem (1994), 38
minority students, problem of environmental disorientation of , 50
multiple and interrelated sources influence valued outcomes, 42
Multiple institution studies of student learning and personal
        development, 11

N
National Study of Student Learning, 11
Nora and Rendon (1990), 22

O
orientation

Penn State receives less than 15 percent of funds from state
        appropriations, 1
Perry's 1970 scheme of intellectual and ethical development, 27
person-environment interaction frameworks, 12
"potent" colleges, xii
practical competence, 25
        out-of-class activities associated with, 39
        student-faculty contact effect on, 40
President of University, ways to foster student learning outside of
        classroom by, 77
process indicators, importance in integration of out-of-class
        learning experiences, 56

Q
questions being answered by this report, 9

R
racial or cultural awareness workshops, 34
Radcliffe College, 51
reflection, encouragement of students, 95
Regester, Joyce, xv
religious faith enhances educational objectives when attending
        affiliated institution, 16
residence halls, programs for students in, 87
Residential living most influential in fostering cognitive growth, 28

S
self-esteem, definition of, 35
Serow and Dreyden (1990), 31
single-sex institution enhances persistence and educational
        attainment, 16
social activities gains in values, self-understanding, teamwork, and
        health, 38–39
social integration from peer-peer interaction and faculty-student
        interaction, 20
social leadership activities relationship to humanitarian and civic
        values, 34
social service ethos requiring student to engage in designated
        activities, 90
Springer et al. (1995), 30
Stoecker and Pascarella (1991) size negatively related to social
        activities, 14–15

student affairs staff fostering student learning outside of classroom, 90–91

key role in promoting student involvement, 83–84

should set expectations for student involvement and standards outside of class, 85

student culture, influence on academic life of, 73

student egalitarian attitude toward women, faculty with liberal attitudes promotes, 37

Student-faculty contact and knowledge acquisition, 32

associated with leadership, social activism, and intellectual self-esteem, 37

benefits depend upon student and institution, 22

Student Learning Project Work Group, xv

students

motivation key task for all institutions, 100

persistence influenced by ratio of student development professionals to students, 23

satisfaction related to confidence in academic abilities and relevant courses, 19

time and effort important for studying learning process, 56

ways to foster student learning outside of classroom by, 93

subcultures on college campus, need to study different effects of, 97

Syracuse University, 3

T

talent development holistic approach for undergraduate education, 66–67

teaching approaches effective in fostering higher levels of learning, 54–55

Terenzini et al. (1995), 30, 31

Terenzini, Springer, Pascarella, and Nora (1994), 30, 42

Test of Thematic Analysis, 28

The Sierra Project, 38

Thompson, Samiratedu, and Rafter (1993), 16

Tidball (1980, 1986), 41

Tidball and Kistiakowsky (1976), 41

Tinto's (1975) model of student attrition, 20

Townsend, Newell, and Wiese (1992), xiii

traditional-age students, programs for parents of, 88

Treisman (1992), 50

U

undergraduate education
>institutional affluence not a critical factor in, 3
>key restructuring questions, 3

University of California, Berkeley, xii, 50, 95

University of California, Irvine, 38

University of Michigan less than 15 percent of operating funds from state, 1

University of Missouri at Columbia, 73

University of Oregon state support in 1995-96 expected to be about 8 percent, 1

V

Volkwein, King, and Terenzini (1986), 30, 42

W

Watson-Glaser Critical Thinking Appraisal, 29

Weidman (1984), 40

Weis (1985), 74

Whiteley and Yokota (19880, 38

Wilson (1992), 51

Wingspread Group (1993), 51
>called for higher expectations for student performance, 5
>challenge to put learning first, 3

Winter, McClelland, and Stewart (1981), 28

Wolfe (1993), 24

women
>activities involvement link to career-development and vocational success, 40–41
>attribute interpersonal competence to contact beyond the classroom, 37
>respond positively to environments that emphasize relational qualities, 20

women's college graduates more likely to enter male-dominated fields, 41

Y

Yankelovich, Daniel, 1

ASHE-ERIC HIGHER EDUCATION REPORTS

Since 1983, the Association for the Study of Higher Education (ASHE) and the Educational Resources Information Center (ERIC) Clearinghouse on Higher Education, a sponsored project of the Graduate School of Education and Human Development at The George Washington University, have cosponsored the ASHE-ERIC Higher Education Report series. The 1994 series is the twenty-third overall and the sixth to be published by the School of Education and Human Development at the George Washington University.

Each monograph is the definitive analysis of a tough higher education problem, based on thorough research of pertinent literature and institutional experiences. Topics are identified by a national survey. Noted practitioners and scholars are then commissioned to write the reports, with experts providing critical reviews of each manuscript before publication.

Eight monographs (10 before 1985) in the ASHE-ERIC Higher Education Report series are published each year and are available on individual and subscription bases. To order, use the order form on the last page of this book.

Qualified persons interested in writing a monograph for the ASHEERIC Higher Education Reports are invited to submit a proposal to the National Advisory Board. As the pre-eminent literature review and issue analysis series in higher education, we can guarantee wide dissemination and national exposure for accepted candidates Execution of a monograph requires at least a minimal familiarity with the ERIC database, including Resources in Education and current Index to Journals in Education. The objective of these Reports is to bridge conventional wisdom with practical research. Prospective authors are strongly encouraged to call Dr. Fife at 800-773-3742.

For further information, write to
ASHE-ERIC Higher Education Reports
The George Washington University
1 Dupont Circle, Suite 630
Washington, DC 20036
Or phone (202) 296-2597, toll free: 800-773-ERIC.
Write or call for a complete catalog.

ADVISORY BOARD

Barbara E. Brittingham
University of Rhode Island

Mildred Garcia
Montclair State College

Rodolfo Z. Garcia
North Central Association of Colleges and Schools

James Hearn
University of Georgia

Bruce Anthony Jones
University of Pittsburgh

L. Jackson Newell
Deep Springs College

Carolyn Thompson
State University of New York-Buffalo

CONSULTING EDITORS

Robert J. Barak
State Board of Regents, Iowa

E. Grady Bogue
The University of Tennessee

John M. Braxton
Vanderbilt University

John A. Centra
Syracuse University

Robert A. Cornesky
Comesky and Associates, Inc.

Peter Ewell
National Center for Higher Education Management Systems

John Folger
Institute for Public Policy Studies

Leonard Goldberg
University of Richmond

George Gordon
University of Strathclyde

Jane Halonen
Alverno College

Dean L. Hubbard
Northwest Missouri State University

Thomas F. Kelley
Binghamton University

Daniel T. Layzell
University of Wisconsin System

Marsha B. Baxter Magolda
Miami University

Laurence R. Marcus
New Jersey Department of Higher Education

Keith Miser
Colorado State University

L. Jackson Newell
University of Utah

James Rhem
The National Teaching & Learning Forum

Gary Rhoades
University of Arizona

G. Jeremiah Ryan
Harford Community College

Karl Schilling
Miami University

Charles Schroeder
University of Missouri

Lawrence A. Sherr
University of Kansas

Patricia A. Spencer
Riverside Community College

David Sweet
OERI, U.S. Dept. of Education

Barbara E. Taylor
Association of Governing Boards

Sheila L. Weiner
Board of Overseers of Harvard College

Wesley K. Willmer
Biola University

Manta Yorke
Liverpool John Moores University

REVIEW PANEL

Charles Adams
University of Massachusetts-Amherst

Louis Albert
American Association for Higher Education

Richard Alfred
University of Michigan

Henry Lee Allen
University of Rochester

Philip G. Altbach
Boston College

Marilyn J. Amey
University of Kansas

Kristine L. Anderson
Florida Atlantic University

Karen D. Arnold
Boston College

Robert J. Barak
Iowa State Board of Regents

Alan Bayer
Virginia Polytechnic Institute and State University

John P. Bean
Indiana University-Bloomington

John M. Braxton
Peabody College, Vanderbilt University

Ellen M. Brier
Tennessee State University

Barbara E. Brittingham
The University of Rhode Island

Dennis Brown
University of Kansas

Peter McE. Buchanan
Council for Advancement and Support of Education

Patricia Carter
University of Michigan

John A. Centra
Syracuse University

Arthur W. Chickering
George Mason University

Darrel A. Clowes
Virginia Polytechnic Institute and State University

Deborah M. DiCroce
Piedmont Virginia Community College

Cynthia S. Dickens
Mississippi State University

Sarah M. Dinham
University of Arizona

Kenneth A. Feldman
State University of New York-Stony Brook

Dorothy E. Finnegan
The College of William & Mary

Mildred Garcia
Montclair State College

Rodolfo Z. Garcia
Commission on Institutions of Higher Education

Kenneth C. Green
University of Southern California

James Hearn
University of Georgia

Edward R. Hines
Illinois State University

Deborah Hunter
University of Vermont

Philo Hutcheson
Georgia State University

Bruce Anthony Jones
University of Pittsburgh

Elizabeth A. Jones
The Pennsylvania State University

Kathryn Kretschmer
University of Kansas

Marsha V. Krotseng
State College and University Systems of West Virginia

George D. Kuh
Indiana University-Bloomington

Daniel T. Layzell
University of Wisconsin System

Patrick G. Love
Kent State University

Cheryl D. Lovell
State Higher Education Executive Officers

Meredith Jane Ludwig
American Association of State Colleges and Universities

Dewayne Matthews
Western Interstate Commission for Higher Education

Mantha V. Mehallis
Florida Atlantic University

Toby Milton
Essex Community College

James R. Mingle
State Higher Education Executive Officers

John A. Muffo
Virginia Polytechnic Institute and State University

L. Jackson Newell
Deep Springs College

James C. Palmer
Illinois State University

Robert A. Rhoads
The Pennsylvania State University

G. Jeremiah Ryan
Harford Community College

Mary Ann Danowitz Sagaria
The Ohio State University

Daryl G. Smith
The Claremont Graduate School

William G. Tierney
University of Southern California

Susan B. Twombly
University of Kansas

Robert A. Walhaus
University of Illinois-Chicago

Harold Wechsler
University of Rochester

Elizabeth J. Whitt
University of Illinois-Chicago

Michael J. Worth
The George Washington University

RECENT TITLES

1994 ASHE-ERIC Higher Education Reports

1. The Advisory Committee Advantage: Creating an Effective Strategy for Programmatic Improvement
   Lee Teitel

2. Collaborative Peer Review: The Role of Faculty in Improving College Teaching
   Larry Keig and Michael D. Waggoner

3. Prices, Productivity, and Investment: Assessing Financial Strategies in Higher Education
   Edward P. St. John

4. The Development Officer in Higher Education: Toward an Understanding of the Role
   Michael J. Worth and James W. Asp, II

5. The Promises and Pitfalls of Performance Indicators in Higher Education
   Gerald Gaither, Brian P. Nedwek, and John E. Neal

6. A New Alliance: Continuous Quality and Classroom Effectiveness
   Mimi Wolverton

7. Redesigning Higher Education: Producing Dramatic Gains in Student Learning
   Lion F. Gardiner

8. Student Learning Outside the Classroom: Transcending Artificial Boundaries
   George D. Kuh, Katie Branch Douglas, Jon P. Lund, and Jackie Ramin-Gyurnek

1993 ASHE-ERIC Higher Education Reports

1. The Department Chair: New Roles, Responsibilities and Challenges
   Alan T. Seagren, John W. Creswell, and Daniel W. Wheeler

2. Sexual Harassment in Higher Education: From Conflict to Community
   Robert O. Riggs, Patricia H. Marred, and JoAnn C. Cutting

3. Chicanos in Higher Education: Issues and Dilemmas for the 21st Century
   Adalberto Aguirre, Jr., and Ruben O. Martinez

4. Academic Freedom in American Higher Education: Rights, Responsibilities, and Limitations
   Robert K. Posh

5. Making Sense of the Dollars: The Costs and Uses of Faculty Compensation
   Kathryn M. Moore and Marilyn J. Amey

6. Enhancing Promotion, Tenure and Beyond: Faculty Socialization as a Cultural Process
   William C. Tierney and Robert A. Rhoads

7. New Perspectives for Student Affairs Professionals: Evolving Realities, Responsibilities and Roles
   Peter H. Garland and Thomas W. Grace

8. Turning Teaching Into Learning: The Role of Student Responsibility in the Collegiate Experience
   Todd M. Davis and Patricia Hillman Murrell

1992 ASHE-ERIC Higher Education Reports

1. The Leadership Compass: Values and Ethics in Higher Education
   John R. Wilcox and Susan L. Ebbs

2. Preparing for a Global Community: Achieving an International Perspective in Higher Education
   Sarah M. Pickert

3. Quality: Transforming Postsecondary Education
   Ellen Earle Chaffee and Lawrence A. Sherr

4. Faculty Job Satisfaction: Women and Minorities in Peril
   Martha Wingard Tack and Carol Logan Patitu

5. Reconciling Rights and Responsibilities of Colleges and Students: Offensive Speech, Assembly, Drug Testing, and Safety
   Annette Gibbs

6. Creating Distinctiveness: Lessons from Uncommon Colleges and Universities
   Barbara K. Townsend, L. Jackson Newell, and Michael D. Wiese

7. Instituting Enduring Innovations: Achieving Continuity of Change in Higher Education
   Barbara K. Curry

8. Crossing Pedagogical Oceans: International Teaching Assistants in U.S. Undergraduate Education
   Rosslyn M. Smith, Patricia Byrd, Gayle L. Nelson, Ralph Pat Barrett, and Janet C. Constantinides

1991 ASHEERIC Higher Education Reports

1. Active Learning: Creating Excitement in the Classroom
   Charles C. Bonwell and James A. Eison

2. Realizing Gender Equality in Higher Education: The Need to Integrate Work/Family Issues
   Nancy Hensel

3. Academic Advising for Student Success: A System of Shared Responsibility
   Susan H. Frost

4. Cooperative Learning: Increasing College Faculty Instructional Productivity
   David W. Johnson, Roger T. Johnson, and Karl A. Smith

5. High School-College Partnerships: Conceptual Models, Programs, and Issues
   Arthur Richard Greenberg

6. Meeting the Mandate: Renewing the College and Departmental Curriculum
   William Toombs and William Tierney

7. Faculty Collaboration: Enhancing the Quality of Scholarship and Teaching
   Ann E. Austin and Roger G. Baldwin

8. Strategies and Consequences: Managing the Costs in Higher Education
   John S. Waggaman

1990 ASHE-ERIC Higher Education Reports

1. The Campus Green: Fund Raising in Higher Education
   Barbara E. Brittingham and Thomas R. Pezzullo

2. The Emeritus Professor: Old Rank New Meaning
   James E. Mauch, Jack W. Birch, and Jack Matthews

3. "High Risk" Students in Higher Education: Future Trends
   Dionne J. Jones and Betty Collier Watson

4. Budgeting for Higher Education at the State Level: Enigma, Paradox, and Ritual
   Daniel T. Layzell and Jan W. Lyddon

5. Proprietary Schools: Programs, Policies, and Prospects
   John B. Lee and Jamie P. Merisotis

6. College Choice: Understanding Student Enrollment Behavior
   Michael B. Paulsen

7. Pursuing Diversity: Recruiting College Minority Students
   Barbara Astone and Elsa Nuñez-Wormack

8. Social Consciousness and Career Awareness: Emerging Link in Higher Education
   John S. Swift, Jr.

1989 ASHE-ERIC Higher Education Reports

1. Making Sense of Administrative Leadership: The 'L' Word in Higher Education
   Estela M. Bensimon, Anna Neumann, and Robert Birnbaum

2. Affirmative Rhetoric, Negative Action: African-American and Hispanic Faculty at Predominantly White Universities
   Valora Washington and William Harvey

3. Postsecondary Developmental Programs: A Traditional Agenda with New Imperatives
   Louise M. Tomlinson

4. The Old College Try: Balancing Athletics and Academics in Higher Education
   John R. Thelin and Lawrence L. Wiseman

5. The Challenge of Diversity: Involvement or Alienation in the Academy?
   Daryl G. Smith

6. Student Goals for College and Courses: A Missing Link in Assessing and Improving Academic Achievement
   Joan S. Stark, Kathleen M. Shaw, and Malcolm A. Lowther

7. The Student as Commuter: Developing a Comprehensive Institutional Response
   Barbara Jacoby

8. Renewing Civic Capacity: Preparing College Students for Service and Citizenship
   Suzanne W. Morse